Dream Season:
Worldwide Guide to Heli & Cat Skiing/Boarding

Bill Wanrooy
Chris Anthony

© 2006 by Karma Publishing, LLC, excluding:
© 2006 by Chris Anthony, pages: 1-3, 28-35, 49-50.
© 2006 by Patrick Crawford, pages: 20-27.
© 2006 by James Morland, pages: 16-18
© 2006 by Bill Wanrooy, pages: 6-8, 43-48.
All rights reserved.

Printed in the United States of America.

Preface

Thank you very much for picking up a copy of Dream Season. I hope you enjoy reading it as much as we enjoyed gathering all the information. We have included all of the operators that we could get into contact with, but inevitably we probably missed a few. As we work on future editions, we plan to continue to make this guide as comprehensive as possible. In the meantime, if you are interested in giving us your feedback or sharing an experience, please contact us at: info@karmapublishing.com. Beware: if skiing is a gateway drug, then heliskiing is a narcotic.

--Bill Wanrooy

Acknowledgements

A special thank you goes out to all the heli and snowcat operators who helped to make this book a reality.

Cover Photo by: Vino Anothony

Contents

I	Introduction to Helicopter Skiing	1
II	Tips for the Ultimate Ski Trip	4
III	Firsthand Experience: Alpine Heli-Ski	6
IV	Firsthand Experience: Kamchatka, Russia	16
V	Firsthand Experience: Mica Heli Guides	20
VI	Firsthand Experience: Monarch Cat Skiing	25
VII	Alaska	28
VIII	Canada	43
IX	Europe & Eastern Europe	82
X	Greenland	92
XI	Himalayas	95
XII	New Zealand	100
XIII	South America	110
XIV	Western United States	113
XV	Index	127

1

Introduction to Helicopter Skiing

I will never forget the sensation of the first time the skids left the ground. It was something I had never experienced before. The feeling was surreal. I was sitting in the front seat next to the pilot as he pulled the collective and angled the stick to the right. The low power Bell helicopter tilted and we accelerated down the valley over the frozen river to gain some momentum before we actually started gaining altitude. The Chugach Mountain Range surrounded us in all its brilliance. My heart was pounding through my chest and I had a smile plastered on my face that has been stuck there ever since. I had never seen anything like it - paradise I thought to myself, with miles of terrain just calling to us. I had no idea where we were going and the pilot had no idea where we wanted to go. But since I had somehow ended up in the front seat it was up to me to pick which peak we would land on.

When I say we, I mean myself and the four strangers located behind the pilot and I in the backseat. I had met them on the road while hitchhiking from Valdez up and over Thompson Pass to the Tsania truck stop (Now known as the Tsania Lodge). We shook hands and formed a group; all of us paid the pilot $50 so he would take us to any one of the peaks we could see from the highway. We didn't have a guide, beacons, shovels, probes or anything that resembled phat skis. These were the cowboy days of Valdez, Alaska. This was my introduction to helicopter skiing and the beginning of an addiction that has been hard to break since.

It has changed in Valdez dramatically since those days and ever since Doug Coombs posted up a cardboard sign that said you could hire him as a guide. Doug eventually went on to found Valdez Heli Ski Guides and Alaska evolved to establish operations not only in Valdez but also in Girdwood, Cordova and Haines. Thanks to the foresight of people like Trevor Petterson, Eric Pehota, Kirk Jensen, Mike Cozad, Scot Schmidt, Craig Kelly, Dave Hamre, Mike Overcast, Dean Cummings, Sean Dog, Dean Conway, Kevin Quinn, Frank Coffey and so many other parts of this family, Alaska was open to for skiing and boarding.

The same thing happened in Canada many years prior to Alaska. Now the Canadian operations set the standard for helicopter skiing. I have only had the opportunity to visit one of them. Mike Wiegeles during its 30th Anniversary and again for a Warren Miller shoot a couple years later. Wiegeles in Blue River British Columbia is the crème de le crème of helicopter skiing, and by all standards an operation that any service oriented operation should base themselves off of when it comes to hospitality and customer service.

Helicopter skiing is a life changing experience. There is nothing like stepping out of a helicopter with a few friends on top of an untracked peak and skiing as much vertical in one shot that would make up that of most large ski resorts top to bottom. It is a sport of adventure, mental growth, bonds, and beauty. Heli Skiing also takes a tremendous amount of preparation and in some places patience. But as they say, anything in life that is hard to achieve is probably worth waiting for.

This book will hopefully alleviate some of the questions about operations, locations and equipment. I will contribute from my first hand experiences at a number of operations while others will give theirs.

INTRODUCTION TO HELICOPTER SKIING

This is info for the rare breed that likes to live everyday for what it is really about!

Chris Anthony
Chris Anthony Adventures
Veteran of Warren Miller Films

2

Tips for the Ultimate Ski Trip

Planning your first heli experience is one of the most exciting things you can possibly do. There is nothing quite like the anticipation that builds as you get closer to your date with destiny. Here are a few things to keep in mind as you evaluate options and plan your dream season.

Choose a trip that is well within your budget. This is very important as the price you are quoted most likely won't be the final price. There are other costs which must be taken into consideration such as extra vertical, tipping, equipment, alcoholic beverages, etc. It is very important to speak with the operator ahead of time in regards to these items. Please note that prices listed in this book are in local currency unless otherwise stated and based on the latest information available before printing.

Extra vertical is something that is very important to consider when looking at the costs of a trip. It can account for a very large expense or no expense at all. This is totally dependent on the weather, but you want to make sure that you are ready to shell out the dough if you have bluebird days. Once you are out in the freshies, there is no way that you will want to cut your day short due to hitting your vertical quota.

Tips for the Ultimate Ski Trip

While on a trip, you will want to ski as much vertical you can get under your belt.

Another key consideration is budgeting so that you can tip your guides. These guides work their asses off in order to find you the best terrain and a significant portion of their income is dependent on tips. Your guides will take good care of you during your heli-skiing vacation; it is your responsibility to take care of them as you head back into the real world.

The gear you bring can play a vital role in the enjoyment of your trip. Remember to use powder skis or boards as they provide a painless adjustment to deep powder. Most operators either rent these or provide them free of charge. Other items needed are high quality goggles, two pairs of gloves, multiple layers of clothing, and casual wear for your time in the lodge. In most instances you will be provided the necessary avalanche gear, with operators preferring you to use the equipment that they provide.

When researching operators, it is important to distinguish between agencies and the actual operators. There are a few agencies that sell heli packages to well known operations. In most instances pricing will be the same either way, but it is important to do your homework.

3

Firsthand Experience: Alpine Heli-Ski

Alpine Heli-Ski Ltd., July 2006
Queenstown, New Zealand

Regardless of which hemisphere you reside in, there is nothing quite like a trip to New Zealand to get your skiing fix from July – October. My fix came on July 14th after a few days of waiting for the weather to cooperate.

I was picked up in the morning at my hotel and brought to a heli pad near the town of Glenorchy. This is not an area that is skied on a very regular basis, but it was where the best snow for the day was. Alpine Heli-Ski has a wide variety of terrain, which enables them to tailor each day's terrain to what Mother Nature dishes out. In only their second year of business, Alpine has been able to secure an impressive amount of terrain through both traditional and creative routes. Sometimes this means securing land rights from farmers through a barter system including heli time, whiskey, beer, wine, and rides to rugby games.

Alpine Heliski operates in NZ's stunning Southern Alps surrounding the international resort towns of Queenstown and Wanaka, with exclusive access to over 2000 square kilometers of exceptional bowls, snowy ridges and powder basins. The terrain spans numerous mountain ranges all offering something unique, and all affected differently by prevailing snow and weather conditions. It is these variations that allow the customization to suit your skill & experience level, minimize your risk, and maximize your powder adventure.

The snow conditions for our day were excellent, with around 45 cm of fresh snow on top of a base of 1.5 meters. Our first three runs were spent in a nice low-angle bowl on Mt. Larkins. There was plenty of deep powder as our guide Woody led us to all the best stashes. Mt. Larkins was a great spot to spend the first half of the day, as the group warmed up for some more challenging terrain. The fourth run was a bit more challenging as there was quite a bit of exposed rock and suspect snow cover. Halfway down the fourth run, we stopped for lunch. The helicopter dropped off a gourmet lunch for us as we took in the breathtaking panorama before us.

After lunch, we skied almost all the way to the valley floor where we were picked up and brought to another peak. Here we found deep snow and wide open terrain. We were able to rip down this run, with everyone smiling from cheek to cheek. At the bottom of the run I asked Woody if he had ever been to the peak next to us, which was a thing of beauty. He said no, but that he had it in mind too. Our next ride in the heli took us there as our last hurrah to cap off the day. After a smooth landing on a steep ridge, we were on the most amazing terrain of the day. It was everything you could ever dream of in a heli trip: steep, deep, and long enough to make your legs feel like they were blazing.

When we arrived back at the heli pad, there were cold beers waiting for us as we concluded one of the best days of skiing anyone could hope for. There were many comments among the group in regards to this being the best day of skiing/boarding in a lifetime.

Alpine Heli-Ski is an extremely professional organization which has become one of Queenstown's premier operators in just its second year in business. This is due to the extreme competency of their staff. The guides have decades of local and international experience between them – not just in heli-ski guiding, but in all aspects of alpine mountaineering. All guides are certified to NZ industry standards; however they have even tighter requirements than the NZ industry code. All senior guides are level 2 avalanche certified; this is the highest avalanche certification available in NZ and is only achieved after many years of field training and study. The Guiding Director position is held by a NZMGA fully certified ski guide. This qualification is the highest Heliski/board guide qualification available in NZ.

For those looking for the most intimate experience, Private Charter allows you to board at your own pace. For expert skiers/riders this means heading into the steep & deep or for more intermediate skiers/riders you can be set down on smooth easy angled powder bowls where you can ski as much or as little as you like. It is possible to ski between 10 and 14 runs, and if your energy is still high after that, then extra helicopter time is available to enable you to ski/ride up to 20 of the longest runs your legs are ever likely to feel.

Bill Wanrooy
July 14, 2006

FIRSTHAND EXPERIENCE: ALPINE HELI-SKI

Alpine Heliski, New Zealand

Dream Season

Alpine Heliski, New Zealand

FIRSTHAND EXPERIENCE: ALPINE HELI-SKI

Alpine Heliski, New Zealand

Dream Season

Alpine Heliski, New Zealand

FIRSTHAND EXPERIENCE: ALPINE HELI-SKI

Alpine Heliski, New Zealand

DREAM SEASON

Alpine Heliski, New Zealand

FIRSTHAND EXPERIENCE: ALPINE HELI-SKI

Alpine Heliski, New Zealand

4

Firsthand Experience: Kamchatka

Kamchatka Peninsula, April 2006
Kamchatka, Russia

During the last ten days of April I was lucky enough to travel to the Kamchatka peninsula in the far east of Russia and experience what will always stand out as one of my most extraordinary memories on skis. This is something totally unique – and not just because our hotel offered, "deep purgation procedure". It may not be everyone's cup of tea but, for those with a strong sense of adventure and an even stronger tolerance for hard booze and putting up with the inevitable waiting that is synonymous with Russia; you cannot help but be blown away.

The landscape is vast on a scale that is impossible to describe and at times you feel as if you have been transported to an entirely different universe. We skied into the craters of smoking, active volcanoes; down to deserted beaches where we swam in the Pacific Ocean, and to wild hot springs for a soak and a bottle of Russian champagne. How we found the energy I will never know, but most days were rounded off with a few moves on the dance floor of the legendary Cosmic nightclub. This place has to be seen to be believed.

Firsthand Experience: Kamchatka

The capital of Kamchatka, Petropavlovsk is a grim city to say the least but its ugliness is offset by the friendliness of the residents and the awesome spectacle of the landscapes that surround it. Never have I seen so many jaws drop with complete sensory overload. At times it was hard to link more than five or six turns before I was compelled to stop and gawp at the surroundings.

On its day, the skiing and riding in Kamchatka is hard to beat but I cannot emphasize enough that no matter how good the conditions may be the skiing or riding is only a fraction of what makes the experience. Many of the runs are typified by endless run outs where you just sit back and relax for three or four miles and take in the dramatic scenery around you. Averaging 1300-1400 meters with descents of up to 4,000 meters the runs are long by any standards, not to mention varied and exciting. If there are any negative sides to skiing here it is perhaps that the weather can be particularly harsh and unpredictable. The peninsula is exposed to ferocious winds that scream in from the Pacific Ocean transforming smoky powder into breakable crust and rock hard boiler plate in a matter of hours.

Looking out of the window on the flight into Petropavlovsk, it was evident that one such wind had recently been blowing. Every single aspect looked like solid concrete! Amazingly, we still managed to find plenty of good powder, and in between we skied some exceptional spring snow, some sparkling surface hoar, cold, dry chalky snow, sun crust, wind crust, rimmed boiler plate and everything in between. You name it, we skied it. All in all the vast majority of runs were on very good snow. There was not a breath of wind for our first five days, and we did not see a cloud. In fact the weather could not have been more perfect. Things changed quickly on day six/seven when a fierce storm came barreling in across the Pacific and battered the peninsula for the next week dumping meters of snow on the surrounding mountains. In our exhausted state this was almost welcome and we spent the next few days exploring the city, visiting the market, skiing at the local resort, lounging in hot springs and recovering from all-nighters in the Cosmic nightclub.

Dream Season

Elemental Adventure who arranged my trip, specialize in organizing heliski trips to the Kamchaka Peninsula and over twelve other locations around the world.

James Morland
Elemental Adventure Ltd
Heliskiing Worldwide
+44 (0)870 738 7838
info@eaheli.com
www.eaheli.com

Firsthand Experience: Kamchatka

5

Firsthand Experience: Mica Heli Guides

Mica Heli Guides, February 2006
Mica Creek, BC Canada

Mica Lodge is a three-year-old newcomer of an operation sitting squarely in middle of the birthplace of heliskiing. The lodge sits on the western slope of the Canadian Rockies, just across the Columbia River from the legendary Selkirk and Monashee ranges. Southeast of Mica are the Bugaboos and the Cariboos, where in 1965 an Austrian mountain guide named Hans Gmoser first improved upon the trusty chairlift by shuttling skiers around inherently dangerous, unpredictable mountain terrain in a million-dollar aircraft. Thanks to Gmoser, it became a central tenet of the sport that every able-bodied skier was required to max out his credit card and make the pilgrimage to the Canadian Rockies at least once in his life. Then a decade ago, the pro skiers and film crews left the Rockies for the Chugach and the BC Coast Range. Meanwhile these mountains, accessed via the small town of Revelstoke, developed a reputation as a haven for intermediates looking to make figure-eights in low-angle bowls.

But since Mica opened for operations in 20TK, the hype has returned to this historic heliskiing region. The Canadian Rockies don't have

Firsthand Experience: Mica Heli Guides

Alaska's 3,000 vertical-foot faces and the snow doesn't stick to nearly vertical walls here, but somehow I don't believe that the birthplace of heliskiing has lost its importance. So I'm here leading a small crew for Freeskier magazine: Freeskier photo editor Jay Michelfelder, pro skiers Dan Treadway and Hugo Harrison, and myself.

Mica's small, three-story log lodge sits in a small clear cut left by loggers. The Columbia River, dammed into a T-shaped lake here, flows in front of the lodge. Behind it lie the Canadian Rockies and Mica's 1,800 square-mile ski zone, a tenure larger than the entire state of Rhode Island. The mountains are buried under an annual average of 40-60 feet of snow that's a perfect blend of continental cold and coastal stable. The alpine zones are reminiscent of the Alps both in the way they ski and in their appearance, but unlike Europe (or Alaska for that matter), half of Mica's terrain is below treeline. In bad weather, pilots can stay low along the trees and keep flying. In three years of operation, Mica has had less than two total down days.

When the helicopter drops us at the lodge, though, it doesn't look like we'll have to test the trees. We land on Centerfold, a peak deep in the zone that holds perfect sun for shooting photos. The snowpack is incredibly stable and nearly knee-deep, leaving us free to ski anything we want. Dan and Hugo both work lines of a few turns that lead into 30-foot airs. Since I don't have to huck for my paycheck, I ski a line down the peak's shoulder where the snow is softer but there's no air.

We move progressively deeper into the zone for several laps, and then in early afternoon we find the terrain we've been searching for, an unnamed ridgeline with narrow, 50-degree lines closed in by rocks. Hugo drops first, taking two cautious turns on bulletproof snow above a 50-plus-degree face, then suddenly he opens it up into his signature GS-style turns around a rock outcropping and flies into the bowl below. Next Dan drops in and rips along a fin, while huge sloughs of snow cascade over a 20-foot cliff band next to him. Dan and Hugo are still buzzing when we gather below the face a few minutes later. Even for the two of the world's best, Mica has the terrain to challenge.

Dream Season

Most of Mica's runs start with above-treeline alpine skiing, which varies widely in aspect and pitch, but is unwaveringly good. The terrain offers a sense of complexity absent in the Chugach. In Alaska, the runs guests ski are frequently a few thousand vertical feet of completely open, consistent skiing. Those runs are like snow-covered cutting boards tilted upward at 45-degrees. They are absolutely incredible powder skiing and a sense of exposure completely unique in the world. The terrain in the Rockies is far more varied within any single run. It pitches and rolls left and right, drops off steeply then flattens out. Eventually most runs drop into the trees before the pick up zone.

Staying at the Mica lodge feels like a scam. We're used to sleeping on sofas and eating 7-11 hot dogs when we travel. The lodge's ground floor is the dining area, the second story has a TV room and common area, plus a few guest rooms, and our room is upstairs on the third floor.

The Olympics have just started, so after dinner each night everyone rolls upstairs to watch the Games. The lodge holds a dozen guests; in our case it's four Americans, Dan and Hugo representing Canada, two young Norwegians and four guys from Vienna. On TV, Bob Costas repeatedly refers to "the mighty Austrians," which always sends the Austrians into wild cheers. My only consolation for America's pathetic showing in the speed events and the Austrian's usual excellence is that the Norwegians and Canadians don't do anything at all and an unknown Frenchman wins the downhill.

Our second day dawns with the worst news in heliskiing: yesterday's milky skies have given way to snow. In Alaska, we'd open a bottle of whiskey at this point and try to drink it blue, but at Mica the sound of the heli warming up echoes through the dining room right on schedule, at 9 a.m. The morning's first drop is an above-treeline ridge that's relatively clear on the approach, but totally swallowed by clouds by the time we're ready to ski. The first few hundred yards are vertigo-inducing milk. On every turn I pop out of the knee-deep snow to start the turn, not really knowing how far I'll drop before I sink in again. At one point, I look uphill and see Treadway auger into a waist-high bulge in the snow that I can only make out because he's stuck in it. "I thought it went *downhill* right there," he yells.

Soon we hit treeline, at first just widely-spaced tree tops poking out through 12-feet of base. Soon we descend into Mica's tree-skiing zones, which deserve at least the level of respect of the alpine.

The storm settles in and we start spinning tree-laps. Our flights are only about 60 seconds up a wooded ridge to a drop called Wildcat, and the laps take less than 10 minutes on the return. This is mossy, old-growth pine forest, trees spaced so perfectly they seem to have been planted with tree-skiing in mind. Lines are wide for a few turns, then there's a pinch between trees and immediately it opens back up. Pillow-lines from small to nearly unskiable are hidden everywhere. The pitch is steep enough that you can't see very well over many of the pillows. Being accustomed to a thin Colorado snowpack, I'm cautious at first. Soon I realize that it's so deep that as long as you point it straight downhill, you can't make a mistake. Every landing is soft, and when a huge mound of powder occasionally collapses under my weight, I just fall through a waterfall of snow into a pillow-soft landing on something below.

Fog fills the valley again on our last morning. Being from Whistler, Dan and Hugo consider themselves experts on all forms of fog, and declare this to be of the low-lying variety. They are certain that we'll fly out of it as we get up into the zone, and they're right. We start the day on a long east-facing ridge, working the areas that are highlighted by splashes of sun that slip between the high peaks to hit our ridge. Soon the light is completely gone, and we bounce across valley to the most open terrain we've skied. It's incredible, knee-deep at a pitch approaching 40 degrees. Craig, our guide, tells us that he skied this zone last year with a snowboard film crew, and the entire bowl ripped to the ground the night after they skied it. The snow holds, but by the time we've finished a lap, the valley fog has inched its way up and swallowed us. We shuttle back to the lodge, change clothes, catch one last heli ride to the truck, and head for home.

Dream Season

I ride the six hours back to Vancouver with Hugo, watching another dark BC night roll by outside the window and thinking about the trip. The massively exposed, rowdy lines of Coast Range and the Chugach are totally unique in skiing. For film crews with weeks of time to wait out the weather and relationships with guides that allow them to access things guests will never ski, that's as good as skiing gets.

At Mica, though, the good life fits into three-day chunks—much more reasonable for the average schedule and wallet. What little Mica lacks in vertical compared to Alaska is more than compensated for by the trees, the quality of the alpine terrain, and the nearly guaranteed heli-time. Given an open-ended ticket to ski anywhere in the world, I'd gladly head back to Mica, back to BC, back to the birthplace of heliskiing.

Patrick Crawford
Editor-at-Large
Freeskier Magazine

6

Firsthand Experience: Monarch Cat Skiing

Monarch Snowcat Tours, 2006
Monarch, CO USA

Monarch Snowcat Tours is owned and operated by Monarch Ski Area, although apart from two chairlift rides and lunch in the lodge, a cat day here feels as removed from the ski area as tiny Monarch ski area does from the crowds of Colorado's mega-resorts. The resort sits just below the crest of Monarch Pass, and its lifts rise right to the Continental Divide at 11,961 feet. From there, the snowcats shuttle skiers even higher up the divide into the cat skiing zones. A few Colorado resorts have higher lift serviced terrain, but none can top the high-altitude Colorado ambience that hits you when you step out of the cat, even if that alpine atmosphere often comes in the form of a cold wind blasting your face with dry, grainy snow. But, the views are astounding, the shelter of treeline is not far below and the skiing is worthy.

I was certainly thankful for the quick descent into the trees as I hunkered down and waited to drop in on a blustery morning last winter. But Scot Schmidt, my childhood hero, was in our 12-person cat group, and I would have braved any weather to ski with him.

Our first run was a short, open bowl called Dog Heaven. I waited at the top with Scot as each person dropped in one at a time. Scot's turn came, and he hucked off a small cornice — with the trademark crossed skis, of course — landed in soft, shin-deep snow and skied down to the waiting cat. I followed, skiing directly next to his tracks and weaving through widely spaced trees and over a small rollover, then ran it out to the pick-up. The jump was tiny and the line won't exactly make any ski movies, but skiing in Scot's tracks was a highlight I won't soon forget.

We skied fast laps on a variety of dog-themed runs — Dog Leg, Dogs Run Free, Fifi's — all morning. Each was about 700 vertical feet and generally similar in feel. There are a few short chutes to play with, but in general the terrain is forgiving: short laps, wide-open spaces and a moderate pitch.

When the dog zones got tracked, we started moving into the trees. That's when things got more exciting. The lines in zones like North Elysian and Mirkwood are a bit steeper, and the forests are tight trees in the classic Colorado style. There's room enough to turn, but not to make mistakes. Hidden throughout the forests are rock drops and small cliff bands where you can work exciting little one-turn-and-point-it lines. It's great, fun tree skiing to be sure, and since it's accessible only by cat, it never gets skied out.

We returned to the main lodge for a leisurely lunch, then sessioned more of the same for the afternoon. Monarch's runs are short, but it's easy to spin a dozen or more laps in a day, so the vert adds up. And with an average snowfall of 350 inches, there's always good pow hidden somewhere, especially if you're willing to get into the tighter tree lines. I was definitely tired when I settled onto a barstool at Benson's bar in nearby Salida later that evening. And while I was lucky to be able to tip back a few pints with Scot and reminisce about my day with a ski icon, I would have been just as content with a satisfying cat day at Monarch had it been just me and a few friends. Monarch seamlessly blends its small-resort funkiness with an ample amount of snow

Firsthand Experience: Monarch Cat Skiing

and solid, but not spectacular, terrain to create a great introduction to the snowcat experience at a relatively affordable $200 price tag.

However, skiers who've already cut their teeth on the big slopes of the West's legendary resorts may find Monarch's terrain too tame. You could find more challenge off the lifts at the nation's big-name resorts, although Monarch holds it snow for days while those resorts are tracked in a few hours. If you go, skip the slope side hotel and book a room in nearby Salida, which has a great little downtown with several bars and restaurants.

Patrick Crawford
Editor-at-Large
Freeskier Magazine

7

Alaska

I have to be honest about Alaska. It is all or nothing and meant for the advance to expert core skiers or riders. Of course a couple of the operations are trying to increase the odds by establishing base camps further inland where the intermountain climate is cooler and weather patterns are a little more stable. With this comes more of an intercontinental snowpack, which changes the dynamics of why the original big mountain riders head to Alaska.

Bottom line Alaska helicopter operations are ruled completely by Mother Nature. Like most females she can be a little moody so there is no reason to argue with her. Just show up be patient and let her decide when you are going to be rewarded. Good things come to those that cooperate.

When potential clients ask me about skiing in Alaska, I tell them one thing. The most wonderful experiences in life are the most difficult to achieve. They look at me annoyed since they were just asking me about heli skiing and not asking me for life advice. A pause takes place, then I ask a few questions and if I can figure out what type of character they are I will say yes, you should go to Alaska. But, understand you really need to be patient. Then they are really confused and ask me why do people go? I just say one thing. If you get it that day it will change your life. I have been going every year since 1991.

*NOTE: *When picking out an operation, think about the entire package and dollar value. See what meals are involved, how the lodging works, transportation etc... Some places might require you to be very responsible for your own well being (such as dinners) outside the guided ski day, while others are all inclusive. For some this is a nice benefit. For others they would rather have more cohesion in the operation.*

For example, the Valdez operations where everything is so spread out, it might be a very good idea to rent a vehicle. This gives you a little more freedom to fill in the days and get from place to place-in comfort and convenience.

The drive from Anchorage is not that bad if you choose to rent a car there. Or you could rent one in Valdez. You are in Alaska, so take advantage of it and check out the surroundings. Go for a drive.

I run my heli camps out of **Points North in Cordova Alaska,** so I may be a little in favor of the region while describing it here. I chose Points North for a number of reasons. Amongst those, the owner Kevin Quinn and the guides work incredibly well together and with the guests. I also love the base camp location as well as the dynamics within the base camp setting. When it comes down to it, this is just as important as the heli terrain itself.

Cordova is land locked but does have daily flights from Anchorage, Juneau and Seattle. The glacier carved mountains run from the sea to the sky with hundreds of inlets. Cordova lodge sits at the mouth of the Orca River in Prince William Sound with mountains towering around it. The region is made up of lush rain forest, glacier wetlands and the Chugach mountain range. It is not uncommon to be skiing creamy powder one day then walking in a rain forest the next with Northern Lights firing in-between. This is a magical place with a variety of landscapes guided by a staff that wants it as bad as you but will exercise the best judgment.

The theory is Alaska has more stable snow conditions then that of its intercontinental counter parts due to its proximity to the ocean. The Chugach is legendary for offering steep alpine descents and Points North is not shy about trying to get you on these. The helicopters land peaks and do not land in saddles unless they have to. Points North wants to thrill you and charges by the heli hour not the vertical accumulated. They also focus on the expert clientele as each person in the field does wear a harness and should arrive with a little previous backcountry experience. When a Points North guide says no, there is a reason for it. The environment can never be taken for granted. This is one hundred percent Alaska.

Points North has two operations. The base operation is Points North One (PNH1) located in Cordova. I love this place, as both my bed and the clients sit only yards from the helicopter pads in the Orca Lodge. This means they can fire anytime and you can be in the mountains in a matter of moments from getting out of bed.

PNH1 feeds everyone in the cafeteria of the Orca Lodge. This is a flashback to childhood summer camp with your bunkmates. A memory comes to me when professional skier Micah Black (there to shoot with Warren Miller) turned the cafeteria into an arts and crafts studio at midnight. He did this when he realized the next day was going to be a down day and people needed something to help ease the tension. He broke out the glacier ice, liquor he collected while in the zone and some finger paints, thus calling the late hours of painting and drinking "Easel and Ice". The next morning clients walked into the lodge to find all their paintings hung up throughout the cafeteria just like in grade school and just beyond them – blue skies with fresh snow on the peaks in the distance. A day I have incredible memories of.

Clients, guides, cooks and pilots all become a tightly knit family at Points North. Extra curricular activities are organized to keep the mind and body working throughout the week. Crazy stuff adults have long forgotten they are capable of doing are standard downtime activities. Like playing dodge ball or finger painting while other more civilized adults can go fishing, hiking, swimming, or ice climbing. At minimum one can find themselves indulged in good conversation at a local watering hole. All of which add to the experience of a lifetime.

To compensate for the lack of stable weather conditions around PNH1, another operation is being developed called PNH2 - Majestic. A much smaller operation that limits itself to 12 guests per week and of course means a little bit more dollars from the pocket. The bright side of PNH2 is that it operates further inland. The cooler temperatures and location stabilize the weather a bit. The snow is light, which of course means the dynamics of the snow changes (See footnote *). The private lodge and zone are in their infancy and worth looking into.

Chugach Powder Guides (CPG) is located about 40 miles out of Anchorage and is the easiest of the Alaskan operations to reach. What particularly makes CPG nice is its proximity to a major international airport, nice hotel, snowcat operation and ski area. Snow safety expert Dave Hamre, junior national downhill sensation Mike Overcast and Olympic gold Medalist Tommy Moe started CPG in the mid 90s. I had met Hamre while competing in the World Extreme Skiing Championships in Valdez where he was part of the safety crew. He mentioned opening up an operation in Girdwood next to the Alyeska ski resort. He invited former World Champion Kim Reichelm and myself to work with them by bringing our groups in as well as promoting the new location. I was thrilled to work with Hamre along with other names and respected guides such as Frank Coffey, Lel Tone and Virgil Hughes.

Clients of CPG stay at the Alyeska Prince Hotel located at the base of the Alyeska resort. From the hotel a tram extends up the North Face of the Alyeska ski area where there are 45-degree slopes in bounds. If the weather still fails to open up, CPG has a snowcat operation ion to tease the clients with some freshies while waiting for those blue skies. The hotel itself is also very nice with modern rooms, a spa, pool and room service. It is a very relaxing place to enjoy the down days.

Girdwood is the surrounding town, where a variety of restaurants exist. The bonus is being close to the city of Anchorage itself with its museums, movie theaters, and bars.

CPG has access to the steeps but does not mind hitting the open bowl skiing with clients, with plenty to choose from in their zones. I also feel the terrain is less glaciated as compared to the Valdez and Cordova operations.

CPG tends to cater to a slightly different level of rider. They pick up the slack the other operations might ignore a bit. It is a bit less intimidating at CPG.

The operation houses the helicopters away from the hotel so it does take one more step to get to the helicopters and into the field. In some cases clients may take van to a remote base area and fly in from there. Clients are a little bit on their own here with extracurricular activities unless they have a very dynamic guide that chooses to become involved with them and organize the activities.

Their signature program operated by Tommy Moe, Mike Overcast and Jeremy Nobis has a very good reputation. It is called **Kings & Corn** and has been highlighted in a couple of Warren Miller's productions. They can do a bit of corn skiing combined with fishing for Salmon in the Alaskan outback. They operate this further inland and house clients in the Tordillo Mountain Lodge located in the Alaska Range. Just like Cordova this may eliminate some of the unstable weather issues a bit. So they have decided to start winter weeks in the lodge as well. This is a premium product. But this does change the physics of the snowpack as well (See footnote).

* The further inland one moves the less stable the snowpack is. One of the original attractions of Alaska comes from the stable coastal snowpack. Which of course means that one can ski steeper terrain with a higher probability of being safe compared to that of an intercontinental snowpack. On the brighter side the snow is colder so probably lighter.

The Valdez Region is where it all began for Alaskan helicopter skiing. The catalyst behind this arose from the exposure created by the early film crews and a short time later the World Extreme Skiing Championships (WESC) founded by Mike Cozad with the help from the town of Valdez, his girlfriend Shannon Loveland, John and Karen McClune. This sparked an entirely new generation of names and era in skiing. Many of the competitors in those first years of the WESC have gone on to give back to the sport through a variety of vehicles. Most of the original operations have popped up from this group. I have not been in Valdez since the 2000 WESC event, but prior to that I was invited to every WESC since 1991. So I will only highlight a couple of operations with my notes and hopefully get a chance to mention a few names that really kicked things off in Alaska.

Valdez- Heli-Ski-Guides (VHSG) operates out of the Brookside Bed and Breakfast in Valdez and the Tsania Lodge on the Thompson Pass highway 35 miles out of Valdez and is owned by Scott Raynor. The operation is the oldest out of the Valdez companies and was founded in 1993 by the late legend and two time World Champion Doug Coombs. He moved his guiding practice to the Tsania Lodge after Bill Bixby, the lawyer for the World Extremes, and a partner (Lisa Wax) purchased the broken down truck stop on the Thompson Pass highway to fix it up. Doug can be credited with formalizing guided operations in the region. Now VHSG has a whole host of guides with very impressive resumes to choose from.

The **Tsaina Lodge** has a ton of character. The walls have seen a plethora of the ski and snowboard industry icons come through the front door. The location is a bit remote but is situated in the heart of where it all began in Alaska. The classic peaks where Rick Armstrong, Trevor Petersen, Eric Pehota, Kirk Jensen, Scot Schmidt, Jim Conway, Dean Conway, Doug Coombs, David Swanwick, the Deslaurier brothers, Egans, Kristen Ulmer, Wendy Brookbank, Kirsten Kramer, The Zells the Jackson Air Force, TGR, Kent Kreitler, Seth Morrison, Wendy Fisher, Shane McConkey, Chris Davenport, and Noel Lyons with so many others of the original pioneers nailed first descents or made a name for themselves in the surrounding mountains.

They would kick back like cowboys did in the old west and tell stories of their travels or better yet what they had just skied.

From the highway outside the Tsaina lodge one can look up at each individual peak as we did back then and say, I want to land there and ski that. But now it is even better as you can fly beyond those front row descents and discover so much more of the region. We used to just pay for one flight at a time, land a peak and ski back to the road where we would hitchhike back to the Tsaina and fork out another $25 to $50 to Chet Simmons our pilot at the time to do it again. Very different from the elaborate packages we now have in Alaska.

35 miles away is the town of Valdez, a small fishing village that had to be relocated after the original town was destroyed by an earthquake in the sixties. The new town is very industrial as the larger economy comes from the fact the Alaskan pipeline terminates just across the harbor.

There is not a lot going on in this neck of the woods. It is important to learn how to slow down when hitting Valdez. Bring your computer and books. This is really a nice place to learn how to pace between heli days and take in the silence of Alaska. It is also an easy place to charter a fishing boat from a local and check out Prince William Sound and maybe get a glance at a couple of whales.

Scott Raynor the current owner of Valdez Heli Ski Guides gives his clients a choice of which base to stay out of: Tsaina or Brookside.

Access the goods with H20 Heli Ski Guides. This is another operation in Valdez attached to a name that comes with legend, former World Champion Dean Cummings. Cummings started this operation around 1995. I was with him when he said he was going to start it. I was like, no way! Really? He did and he has been kicking butt showing people the Chugach ever since. He even hosted the 2000 World Extreme Championships to a small group of invited athletes in order to show his loyalty while giving back to the sport.

I have skied with Dean in Alaska and of all places Iran. We climbed Mount Damavend together for a Warren Miller production along with 2000 World Champion Spencer Wheately one of Dean's guides. Cummings is a very experienced guide and operator who runs his establishment with a strong arm and intensity. He will put you in the game if you are worthy. If you are capable he is one of the guys in Alaska worth being with. Flying with this operation is full on!

H2O concentration focuses on keeping things small in a massive environment. They have fewer clients on a daily basis than the other operation yet have permits to reach a tremendous amount of acreage. So things can move a little more streamlined in the field as it gives you the sensation of being part of a private program rather than one of the numbers in larger operation. They can fly you out of 9 various remote venues into the Chugach and house everyone at the Best Western on the Valdez Harbor. He will also do non-inclusive days on Fridays and Saturdays if you happen to be in the neighborhood.

Chris Anthony
Chris Anthony Adventures
Veteran of Warren Miller Films

Alaska Operator Directory

Alaska Backcountry Adventures
3037 River Road at Squaw Valley
Tahoe City, CA
USA
888-Swayback
530-581-1767
www.alaskabackcountry.com
info@swayback.com

Year Established: 1991

Terrain Description:

Chosen for the best terrain and longest runs in the Chugach range. This means less distance to fly, which translates into saving hundreds of dollars per day. Location has the best weather patterns of any Alaskan operation with deep maritime snowpack and frequent blue sky.

Range of Trip Durations:

Flexibility to fit any budget from one run to full week packages.

Price Range:

$99 – Single Run.
$675 – Full Day.
$4,000 – Full Week Package, including Lodging.

Alaska Heliskiing
Haines, Alaska
USA
907-767-5745
www.alaskaheliskiing.com
seandog@alaskaheliskiing.com

Price Range: $350 - $3,750.

"Based in Haines, Alaska, Out of bounds specializes in custom helicopter adventures for people of all abilities. Transportation is provided by Coastal Helicopters in state-of-the-art, turbine A-STARS.

Big terrain and first descents are the rule with many runs over 4,000 vertical feet," –www.alaskaheliskiing.com.

Alaska Rendezvous Heli Guides
HCR 90
Valdez, AK 99686
USA
307-734-0721 (Nov. – Jan.)
907-822-3300 (Feb. – Oct.)
www.ARLinc.com
info@ARLinc.com

Year Established: 2000

Season: March – May.

Terrain Description:

Advanced to severe, very long runs, stretching from summits to valleys.

Range of Trip Durations: Up to 7 days.

Price Range: $780/day.

Located in the Chugach Mountains, 50 miles North of Valdez on Thompson Pass. ARL/ARG has more fly days than other location in Alaska.

The staff at ARL/ARG are from the original founding companies in the Thompson Pass/Valdez area. Alaska Rendezvous Guides have banded together to create an atmosphere of friendly unmanipulative business practices utilizing the original big mountain guides and their over 50 years of guiding experience in the great land of Alaska. ARL provides a friendly, warm, and comfortable setting for guests to relax in a home away from home atmosphere, while charging up for another breathtaking day of adventure skiing.

Chugach Powder Guides
PO BOX 641
Girdwood, AK 99587
USA
907-783-HELI
www.chugachpowderguides.com
info@chugachpowderguides.com

Price Range: $850 - $7,250.

"Chugach Adventure Guides (CAG) helicopter operation was founded as Chugach Powder Guides (CPG) in 1997. Alaska was just becoming known on the world scene as a recognized destination for backcountry ski terrain. While the media grabbed onto the hard adventure hype surrounding events like the World Extreme Skiing Championships, we knew the Chugach Range wasn't just for adrenaline junkies. Since then, CPG helicopters have opened up the finest backcountry skiing and boarding in the world, flying guests to adventures that are suitable for all skill levels. We have cataloged over 500 runs and thousands of landings between the pioneering of the Tordrillos and the Chugach. Today, this indescribable terrain and our stellar reputation bring ski and snowboard enthusiasts from around the world to experience mountain adventures that are exclusive to Alaska.

Our terrain and reputation have bought the finest backcountry guides in North America to our door. Being skiers first and foremost, CPG understands that if our clients come all the way to Alaska, it is imperative that they ski or ride no matter what. With this in mind, we developed our snowcat skiing terrain for no-fly days and have fostered a cooperative relationship with Alyeska Resort to assure that you ski or board no matter what, without compromising our safety standards," www.chugachpowderguides.com .

H2O Heli Guides of Alaska
PO BOX 2501
Valdez, AK 99686
USA
907-835-8418
800-578-HELI
www.h2oguides.com
dean@h2oguides.com

Established: 1995

Season: February – April.

Terrain Description:

1.2 million acres of the Chugach. Impeccable safety record and ability to access the goods, speak for itself.

Range of Trip Durations:

Daily, Weekly, and Custom packages available.

Price Range: $850 and up.

Points North Heli-Adventures Inc.
PO BOX 1610
Cordova, AK 99574
USA
877-787-6784
www.alaskaheliski.com

Dream Season

Price Range: $4,975 - $6,250.

"Due to the overwhelming response to our Gold Pass Program, we decided to create the "Big Daddy" of all ski passes. We want you to come and enjoy PNH for a lifetime.

The reason we are the most successful heli-ski operation in Alaska is simple. We access the best terrain in the world, and we provide the most complete lodging experience anywhere in Alaska. Our return rate of over 70% confirms what guests have been saying since the first season: they want to come back forever. Now they can.

We are proud to announce our 3 new Gold Pass options:

For $85K The LIFETIME pass will give you or any person you choose 1 full month of heli time and lodging every year for the rest of your life. Imagine never having a heli bill again. In Canada you can get your own private A-Star for only 1 week at this price.

If one month a year isn't enough for you, The ALL ACCESS pass provides heli time and lodging for the entire season, for life. This pass is $150K.

So you don't want to go alone? Bring a friend or send 2 of your friends for the entire season for unlimited skiing and lodging, for life. Check out the $250K UNLIMITED pass. We have only 1. All of these passes are transferable, so if there's ever a time you can't make it, simply send a couple of friends or anyone you so choose.

We have a very limited number of these passes available so don't wait until they are gone to ask about them. Points North is once again getting ready to reach new heights. As quoted by the man himself, Warren Miller, "If you don't go heli-skiing this year, you will be one year older when you do,"" –www.alaskaheliski.com.

Valdez Heli Camps
PO BOX 2495
Valdez, AK 99686
USA
907-783-3243
907-783-3513
www.valdezhelicamps.com
info@valdezhelicamps.com

Price Range: $275 - $54,999.

"You are standing on top of a jagged, snow-encrusted peak with heart-stopping views of the Alaskan Chugach range in every direction. The sky is bluebird and the morning sun glistens off the champagne powder energizing each snowflake with sparkles of light. Collectively, they summon you. A lone bald eagle soars overhead. Welcome to Alaska. Your life is about to change.

Your guide picks a line and drops in. Watching him rhythmically float through the ocean of fresh snow sends a charge of adrenaline surges through your blood. The ache, the craving that has consumed you for so long has become almost unbearable as you anxiously await your turn. Suddenly, you're up. You have never been more ready for anything in your life.

You drop in. You dance. Space, time and form disappear and are replaced with a life-energy that can only be described as pure, real, CORE. This is life! This is peace. You pull up next to your guide with a breathless exuberance. Your heart is racing, your eyes are ablaze and your soul is alight," --www.valdezhelicamps.com.

Valdez Heli-Ski Guides
PO BOX 57
Girdwood, AK 99587
USA
907-835-4528
www.valdezheliskiguides.com
info@valdezheliskiguides.com

Price Range: $6,450 - $58,000.

"Our heliskiing is unlike anything you could ever imagine. Our ski runs are long and adventurous (up to 5,000 vertical feet), and deep powder is the norm. Group sizes are small (4 clients to 1 guide), allowing us to provide you with a more personalized experience. To those new to big mountain skiing, we offer our terrain progression program. This program is designed to teach you the skills needed to ski big mountains with ease. If you're looking for the next step in skiing or boarding, then VHSG is the place.

Valdez Heli Ski Guides caters to advanced and expert skiers and riders. You don't need to be an extreme skier, but you need to be capable of skiing black diamond terrain in a variety of snow conditions. Your guide will choose the appropriate terrain for you and your group's ability level.

VHSG bases out of the Brookside Bed and Breakfast in Valdez as well as the historic Tsaina Lodge on Thompson Pass, 35 miles from Valdez, Alaska. Weather conditions at our base are more reliable than anywhere else in the Chugach Mountains. In 2003 we experienced only 10 unflyable days! On the days when we can't fly, we offer ski touring, ice climbing, sea kayaking, snow machining as well as halibut and salmon fishing," --www.valdezheliskiguides.com.

8

Canada

On February 8, 2006, as Jeff Jeltema and I prepared to fly into the backcountry lodge, we crossed paths with a group that was just finishing their stay at **Mica Heli Guides**. The first guest off the heli said the trip was, "fucking amazing!" The next guest explained, "this was the best experience of my life!" Finally the last guest let us know, "it was chest deep everyday!" From the looks on everyone's faces, we knew this was going to be one hell of a trip.

In the realm of heli-ski operators, Mica is pretty new, but they seriously have their shit together. There is a reason why you can find an image of their terrain in almost every issue of any ski magazine. The location is also a favorite of visiting film crews, with runs named by Matchstick Productions and Teton Gravity Research.

When you go to Mica, it feels like you are stepping into a ski movie. There is a ton of excellent alpine skiing, plus the best trees you will ever ski. You don't have to be a pro to ski here, but with over a million acres of terrain, they have the goods to challenge the world's best.

In addition to the massive terrain and beautiful fly-in lodge, the groups are small. There are no more than twelve skiers at a time, with 4 per helicopter. This means that you are not going to experience the cattle call that you do at bigger operators. There is no farming of snow, as there is an unlimited supply of powder in this eternal playground.

The accommodations at Mica Heli Lodge are top-notch. The lodge is a beautiful, heli-accessed log cabin with big windows and panoramic views. The meals were excellent, as guests are bound to grow a heli belly during their stay. We spent our evenings watching movies, sending emails, drinking beers, enjoying good conversation, and relaxing in the outdoor hot tub.

Our three days with Mica Heli Guides were all bluebird days, giving us the ultimate ski trip. While staying at Mica, guests don't have to stress about the possibility of down days. Down days at Mica are very rare, with less than 1 per year. This is possible because the lodge sits at a higher elevation than other operators. When other operators are grounded, guest at Mica are enjoying face shots in the trees!

We were able to log 23,200 meters of vertical in our 3 days of skiing with Mica Heli Guides. When looking through the various operators in British Columbia, Mica Heli Guides definitely falls at the top of the list. Every run that I experienced at Mica was the best run of my life. I truly believe that every skier needs to go to Mica at least once and they will find that once isn't nearly enough!

Bill Wanrooy
February 8 – 11, 2006

CANADA

Flying to the Lodge, Mica Heli Guides.

Pickup Time, Mica Heli Guides.

Bill Wanrooy, Mica Heli Guides.

Left to Right: Jeff Jeltema, Bill Wanrooy, and Rob Turner (Guide), Mica Heli Guides.

I have only flown with one operation in Canada and it happened to be the crème de la crème of any operation in the world: Mike Wiegeles Heli operation in Blue River, BC. I was lucky enough to be up there for his 30th anniversary of business and a few years later to shoot a Warren Miller segment.

This is a five star all-inclusive operation with skiing guaranteed in the Monashee or Cariboo ranges of British Columbia. The location is in interior Canada, lower in latitude than where I spend most of my time in Alaska so the tree line is higher, the weather is more consistent and the snow is lighter. Due to those elements, Wiegeles' clients will always be skiing. They won't get the steep like Alaska but you will be skiing glaciers and some of the greatest tree skiing on the planet.

This is not a cowboy show, this is a finely polished Austrian/Canadian run outfit. With employees wandering the customized lodges while polishing, dusting and cleaning in uniform. The base operations are out of this world with catered service on every level. The accommodations and food rivals the best hotels and restaurants in Austria and New York City. I have skied here with client groups made up primarily of intermediate skiers as well as expert, which I thoroughly enjoyed. It showed me that heli skiing is not meant only for the pure expert or extremist but rather for anyone capable of skiing a resort and putting on a pair of phat skis. In fact, one of the women in my group on that fine day was well into her late sixties.

The accommodations are awesome with heli pads just yards from everyone's cabins. Every morning the helicopters come up the valley flying in formation from where they are kept every night. As they approach, they separate and land on their respected pads next to one of the several cabins. Client's skis are brought to the heli pad and loaded by guides, after they are stored and tuned up in a state of the art shop on base.

Wiegeles flies most of the groups in large Bell 212 helicopters unless you ante up for a private A-Star. The 212 holds 10 clients and 2 guides. This means each group has a tail guide. The A-Star is four clients and the guide.

Wiegeles is the sure thing.

Chris Anthony
Chris Anthony Adventures
Veteran of Warren Miller Films

Canada

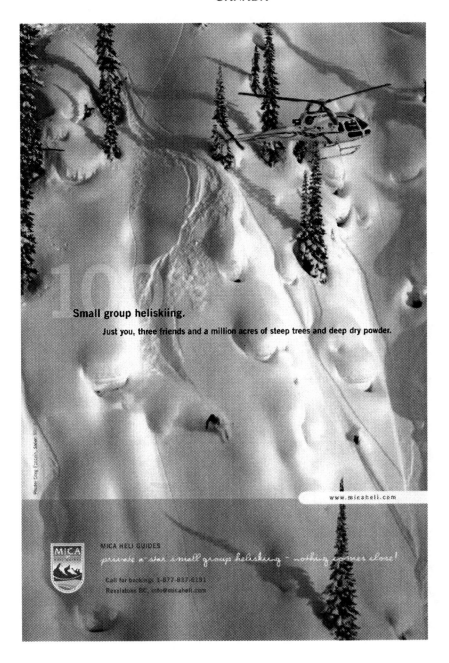

Canada

Canada Operator Directory

Baldface Lodge Snowcat Skiing
PO BOX 906
Nelson, BC
V1L 6A5
Canada
250-352-0006
www.baldface.net
info@baldface.net

Price Range: $450 - $800.

Bella Coola Heli Sports
PO BOX 616
Whistler, BC
V0N 1B0
Canada
604-932-3000
www.bellacoolahelisports.com
www.bigmountainheliskiing.com
info@bellacoolahelisports.com

Year Established: 2000

Season: January – May.

Terrain Description:

Located in Bella Coola, BC, our strength lies in high alpine terrain and majestic scenery with jagged rock towers, giant glacier bowls, and steep couloirs crowned by enormous peaks. Everything from scary steeps to golf course cruising!

Range of Trip Durations:
Trips are: 3day, 4day, 5day, or 7 day Tours.

Price Range: $3,580 to $12,970 per person.

1.5 million acres of wilderness terrain serviced "exclusively" by our fleet of A Star B2 helicopters. Small group sizes with a maximum of only 15 guests per week. Optional Big Mountain Heliskiing tours are discounted tours with the emphasis on the same 'big mountain' heliskiing experience but with an affordable alternative to the main lodge. Get more heliskiing and boarding for your dollar. Our Springs and Corn tours offer big river fishing and corn snow heliskiing during the month of June.

Big Red Cats
Red Resort
PO BOX 802
Rossland, BC
V0G 1Y0
Canada
250-362-2271
www.bigredcats.com
ski@bigredcats.com

Price Range: $199 - $350.

Blackcomb Helicopters Ltd.
PO BOX 1241
Whistler, BC
V0N 1B0
Canada
604-938-1700
www.blackcombhelicopters.com
info@blackcombhelicopters.com
Established: 1989

Terrain Description:
Wide variety of terrain to choose from. Guides determine terrain based on level of experience, weather, and snow conditions.

Price Range:

$6,000 daily for Private Charter:
- 1.5 hours of flight time.
- Professional guide, transceivers, and powder skis.
- Lunch.
- 1 – 4 passengers.

Private charters enable guides to provide more of a personal experience to clients in comparison to the traditional large group experience.

Blomidon Cat Skiing
PO BOX 941
Corner Brook, NF
A2H 6J2
Canada
709-783-2712
709-632-0077
www.catskiing.net
info@catskiing.net

Price Range: $245 - $275 per person, per day.

"The terrain consists of everything from intermediate to extreme slopes. Our experienced guides, equipped with portable radios, will ensure they find suitable terrain and snow conditions for each group. Along with taking all precautions to ensure a high level of safety, we equip all skiers with the latest electronic avalanche transceivers.

The 10-15 minute snow cat rides give you time to relax, clean your goggles, and warm up between runs. Our season runs from mid-December to late April. Whether you come with friends, or are traveling alone, you will find a great time to be had by all." – www.catskiing.net.

Canadian Mountain Holidays
PO BOX 1660
Banff, Alberta
Canada
403-762-7100
www.cmhski.com
info@cmhinc.com

Price Range: $3,402 – $10,272.

Cat Powder Skiing Inc.
PO BOX 1479
Revelstoke, BC
V0E 2S0
Canada
www.catpowder.com
catski@revelstoke.net

Price Range: $500 - $550/day.

Rates include snowcat skiing, meals, and accommodation.

Chatter Creek Cat & Heli Skiing
PO BOX 333
Golden, BC
V0A 1H0
Canada
877-311-7199
www.chattercreek.ca
chatter1@telus.net

Price Range: $1,650 – $5,400.

Coast Range Heliskiing
PO BOX 16
Pemberton, BC
V0N 2L0
Canada
800-701-8744
604-894-1144
604-894-1146 (fax)
www.coastrangeheliskiing.com
jf@coastrangeheliskiing.com

Price Range: $775 – $4,350.

Crescent Spur Helicopter Holidays Ltd.
Crescent Spur, BC
V0J 3E0
Canada
800-715-5532
www.crescentspur.com
info@crescentspur.com

Price Range: $5,530 - $97,900

Dream Catcher Heliskiing Ltd.
PO BOX 452
Vanderhoof, BC
V0J 3A0
Canada

Terrain Description:

Located in the Coast Mountains of Bella Coola, British Columbia.

Price Range: $735 - $13,050 per person.

DREAM SEASON

Eagle Pass Heli Skiing
PO BOX 2555
Revelstoke, BC
V0E 2S0
Canada
877-929-3337
250-837-3734
www.eaglepassheliskiing.com
info@eaglepassheliskiing.com

Range of Trip Durations:

3 & 7 day packages.

Price Range: $3,650 - $15,750.

"We have identified one of the classic heliskiing areas in the world! World class tree and alpine skiing and epic amounts of snow along with owner operators who are highly experienced in the Canadian heliskiing industry will ensure that your B.C. heliskiing adventure exceeds all your expectations," –www.eaglepassheliskiing.com.

Fernie Wilderness Adventures
561B Hwy 3
Fernie, BC
V0B 1M0
Canada
250-423-6704
www.fernieadventures.com
info@fernieadventures.com

Price Range: $300 per person, per day.

CANADA

Great Canadian Heliskiing
PO BOX 175
Golden, BC
V0A 1H0
Canada
250-344-2326
www.greatcanadianheliski.com
info@canadianheli-skiing.com

Price Range: $2,527 - $9,350.

Great Northern Snowcat Skiing
Selkirk Mountains, BC
Canada
403-239-4133
800-889-0765
www.greatnorthernsnowcat.com
info@greatnorthernsnowcat.com

Year Established: 1979

Season: Mid-December – Mid-April

Terrain Description:

Nestled deep in the heart of the Selkirk Mountains of British Columbia, Canada. Private Lodge is located approximately 1.5 hours South of Revelstoke, British Columbia. There is a wide variety of terrain to challenge all abilities.

Range of Trip Durations:

3 or 6 day packages which include skiing, accommodations, & meals at exclusive lodge.

Price Range:
Check website for update prices.

Great Northern Snowcat Skiing is one of the longest continuous snowcat operations in the world – 28 years! Your ski holiday will run effortlessly due to the high standard of organized efficiency. Great Northern Snowcat Skiing makes it look easy, but behind the informality there is a group of very dedicated professionals.

Grizzly Lake Cat Skiing
PO BOX 1034
Sun Peaks, BC
V0E 5N0
Canada
250-578-8982
www.powderhoundscatskiing.com
info@powderhoundscatskiing.com

Price Range: $700 - $1,650.

Highland Powder Skiing
PO BOX 200
Meadow Creek, BC
V0G 1N0
Canada
250-366-4260
www.highlandpowderskiing.com

Price Range: $1,630 - $3,052.

HighSky Adventures
Vernon, BC
V1T 6Y4
Canada
www.highskyadventures.com
inquire@highskyadventures.com

Price Range: $6,200+

CANADA

Island Lake Lodge Catskiing
PO BOX 1229
Fernie, BC
V0B 1M0
Canada
888-422-8754
250-423-3700
www.islandlakelodge.com
reserve@islandlakelodge.com

Price Range: $556 per person, per day. Includes accommodations, all meals, catskiing, & ski/snowboard rental.

Klondike Heliskiing
PO BOX 377
Atlin, BC
V0W 1A0
Canada
800-821-4429
250-651-7474
www.atlinheliski.com
heliski@tirol.com

Price Range: $6,260 - $8,350.

Last Frontier Heliskiing
PO BOX 1118
Vernon, BC
V1T 6N4
Canada
800-655-5566
250-558-7980
www.lastfrontierheli.com
info@lastfrontierheli.com

Price Range: $3,208 - $8,762

Dream Season

Mica Heli Guides
122 MacKenzie Ave.
Revelstoke, BC
V0E 2S0
Canada
877-837-6191
250-837-6191
www.micaheli.com
info@micaheli.com

Year Established: 2002

Terrain Description:

1,000,000+ acres; 50% steep tree skiing, 50% high alpine.

Range of Trip Durations:

Tours come in: 3 day, 4 day, 6 day, 7 day, or 8 day packages.

Price Range: $4,355 to $12,750.

100% small group heli skiing – 4 guests/guide, max 3 groups of 4 creates a very intimate heli ski experience. Powerful A-Star B2 helicopter with small groups can access more terrain and allows Mica Heli to tailor the skiing to the individual group. Remote backcountry lodge, high elevation, and close proximity to world class tree skiing means less weather related down days.

The Western slope of the BC Rockies is a powder making machine. This area is the farthest inland rain forest in the world receiving 13 – 20 meters (40 – 60 feet) of snow annually. Mica Heli is located right where the moist storms from the West collide with the cold arctic air from Northern Alberta. The result is consistent deep dry powder from November to May, with better snow quality in warm weather cycles.

Canada

Mike Wiegele Helicopter Skiing
PO BOX 159
1 Harrwood Drive
Blue River, BC
V0E 1J0
Canada
800-661-9170
250-673-8381
www.wiegele.com
reservations@wiegele.com

Price Range: $3,477 - $11,304.

"For over 35 years Mike Wiegele Helicopter Skiing has been committed to the "soul" of skiing. It has always been more than just a sport, it is a way of life and this will never change," --www.wiegele.com.

Monashee Powder Snowcats
13912 Ponderosa Way
Coldstream, BC
V1B 1A4
Canada
866-678-SNOW
250-545-0661
www.monasheepowder.com
bookings@monasheepowder.com

Price Range: $350 - $650 per person, per day.

"Welcome to Monashee Powder Snowcats. Our goal is to provide enthusiastic powder skiers with a fun and safe holiday in untracked powder. Known throughout the world for having the best tree skiing anywhere, the Monashees are located in the heart of British Columbia's interior Snow Belt.

We ride through the trees, cut blocks and high alpine areas of our terrain. The snowcat transports you up the mountain on "snow roads", drops you off and the guide takes you on a new route through the powder. We try and ski new runs and fresh snow each time the cat drops you off.

For your safety, all our lead guides are either UIAGM or ACMG certified. However, all the risks of backcountry skiing cannot be completely eliminated.

Monashee Powder Snowcats grew out of Monashee Powder Adventures which has been in business since 1998. Monashee Powder developed from a 12 guest, tent operation to a company with two distinct locations and comfortable mountain lodges. The original lodge site at Tsuius Mountain, south of the Trans Canada Highway, is now Monashee Powder Snowcats owned and operated by Tom and Carolyn Morgan. The Lodge is accessed by snowcat, so there is a special meeting place set up on Highway 6, east of Vernon, B.C.

The lodge houses 24 guests plus staff and is on the front edge of the Monashee Mountains, famous for big snowfalls and steep tree skiing. There is also great alpine skiing - on average we spend more than half of our time skiing at 'tree-line' and above."
--www.monasheepowder.com.

Mustang Powder Lodge
Site 23, Comp. 11, RR 2
Chase, BC
V0E 1M0
Canada
888-884-4666
250-679-8125
250-679-2999 (fax)
www.mustangpowder.com
info@mustangpowder.com

Year Established: 1998

Season: Early December – Early April.

CANADA

Terrain Description:

High elevation, remote lodge located Northwest of Revelstoke in the Monashee range. It is 125 sq. km of alpine and sub-alpine terrain. Great old-growth forest tree skiing. Has vast alpine area with glacier. Lots of variety on all different aspects. Located in the Snowbelt of the Monashee Mountains.

Range of Trip Durations:

3 – 5 days. Guests arrive at lodge on the afternoon prior to their holiday dates and ski full days each day. They depart after skiing on the last day of the trip.

Price Range:

$450 - $750 per day. This includes everything: skiing, accommodation, meals, transport to and from lodge, etc.

Massive luxurious timberframe lodge located just below tree-line with spectacular views. Short snowcat rides each morning. Has reliable early-season conditions. Enormous amount of terrain (any bigger and a snowcat couldn't reach the far corners in a day.

Northern Escape Heli-Skiing
PO Box 59
Terrace, BC
V8G 4A2
Canada
250-615-3184
www.NEheliski.com
info@NEheliski.com

Year Established: 2002

Terrain Description:
Exceptionally long glacier runs with incredible tree skiing.

Range of Trip Durations:

3, 4, and 7-day all inclusive vacations.

Price Range:

$2,825 to $7,850

One of the largest Heli-Skiing areas on the planet with a max of 16 guests per week. An intimate and exclusive destination. The way Heli-Skiing and Heli-Boarding were meant to be!

Pantheon Helisports
PO BOX 1461
Squamish, BC
V0N 3G0
Canada
866-404-HELI
604-815-4542
www.pantheonheli.com
info@pantheonheli.com

Range of Trip Durations:

Trips are for: 3 days, 4 days, or 7 days

Price Range: $4,850 - $10,500.

"Pantheon Helisports' half million acres of brand new heli skiing terrain is now ready to explore, complete with thousands of potential first descents. Located between Whistler and Bella Coola, British Columbia, the heli skiing terrain has been a favorite of professional skiers such as Warren Miller Productions for more than a decade. Now for the first time, this big mountain experience is open to those looking for an authentic challenge.

Of the 100 tallest peaks in BC's Coast Mountains, 90 are in the Pantheon Helisports area. The higher elevation riding translates into very long runs (4,000 foot descents are common) and lower moisture content snow than at low-elevation ski areas. In addition, the lodge and terrain is on the east (lee) side of the Coast Mountains, so what you get is a powder experience that has more vertical, more dry snow and more bluebird skies.

Pantheon Helisports is based from the famed White Saddle Ranch, a 1,300-acre working cattle ranch on the edge of the coast wilderness that has been used by mountaineers and skiers as a base for incredible adventures for the past 40 years. The ranch's comfortable cabins are located right next to the hand-carved log lodge, just steps from the helicopter hangar. Relax after a true day of exploration and challenge at an authentic working ranch set amidst world-class heli-skiing terrain that is yours to discover," -- www.pantheonheli.com.

Peace Reach Heli Ski
PO BOX 569
Hudson's Hope, BC
V0C 1V0
Canada
866-575-4354
250-483-4205
www.peacereachheliski.com
info@peacereachadventures.com

Price Range: $8,650 - $57,900.

"My wife Sarah and I first discovered the Peace Reach arm of Williston Lake in the summer of 1985 during one of our excursions through the Northern Rockies of British Columbia.

We kept coming back to this vast, untouched mountain wilderness and soon realized its potential for Heli Ski activities. With an average annual snowfall of 45 feet of dry champagne powder snow, we found the some of the most incredible heli ski terrains in the world.

Dream Season

In 2001 Peace Reach Adventures Ltd., was granted tenure by the Government of British Columbia to conduct Summer and Winter Heli Ski activities in the over 8,000 square kilometers (3,000 square miles) of land along the mountains of the Peace Reach known as the Northern Rocky Mountains.

We have currently developed over 200 Heli Ski runs ranging from outstanding tree runs with over 1100 meters (3700 feet) vertical to majestic wide open powder filled bowles.

We at Peace Reach Heli Ski are dedicated to providing our guests with a very personalized, upscale Heli Ski experience. All of our packages are conducted in a 'small group' environment with 4 skiers /boarders to 1 guide ratio and utilizing roomy A-Star helicopters. This guarantees our guests the flexibility and freedom to ski different terrains at their own pace and enables us to accommodate all levels of expertise and energy levels.

During your winter Heli Ski vacation you will be pampered and cozy at Torwood Lodge. The luxurious Torwood Lodge sits 90 miles west of Fort St. John amidst 300 private acres overlooking Williston Lake in an area known as the 'Serengeti of the North.' Guest rooms are spacious, meals are finely designed for an active winter holiday and the common rooms include a great room an fireplace, whirlpool spa, a fitness room and fully stocked bar!

If you enjoy skiing in the wild, uninhabited mountains of the Northern Rockies, and have sense of adventure and discovery, we invite you to join us for the Heli Ski experience of a lifetime. Heli Ski down from the tops of mountains no one has ever stood on since the beginning of time.join us and experience the Peace Reach difference," –Sarah and Rainer Maas,
www.peacereachheliski.com.

CANADA

Powder Cowboy Catskiing
PO BOX 1229
602a 2nd Ave.
Fernie, BC
V0B 1M0
Canada
888-422-8754
250-423-3700
www.powdercowboy.com
dave@islandlakeresorts.com

Range of Trip Durations:

Trips are: 2days, 3days, or 4 days

Price Range: $952 – $2,700.

"Experience the feeling of untouched powder again and again. Whether you ski or board, the 8-14 daily runs will quickly become your most memorable. As the day ends, you'll have 10,000 to 14,000 vertical feet of bowls, open slopes and awesome tree skiing under your belt with the longest run stretching 2,500 vertical feet. There are 12 guests and 2 guides per snowcat. Saddle up and hold on.

With 3,500 acres of new terrain, Powder Cowboy now boasts 6,000 acres of awesome terrain, equaling the size of many North American ski resorts. And with 350 inches of snowfall a year it's a powder playground for skiers and riders alike," --www.powdercowboy.com.

Powder OutfittersHeli & Cat Ski Adventures
Westbridge, BC
Canada
866-449-2893
250-862-7528
www.powderoutfitters.com
ski@powderoutfitters.com
Price Range: $325 - $2,600.

"We have combined experience, skills, service quality and small group sizes together with the world famous snow of the Monashee Mountains. The combination will forever change your idea of a ski holiday. Our runs average 1,000 to 2,500 vertical feet and only a small portion has been explored. The chance of skiing new runs and naming them still exists." –www.powderoutfitters.com.

Purcell Helicopter Skiing Ltd.
PO Box 1530
Golden, BC
V0A 1H0
800-HELISKI (800-435-4754)
250-344-5410
www.purcellhelicopterskiing.com
info@purcellhelicopterskiing.com

Year Established: 1973

Terrain Description:

Varied terrain offering different levels of abilities for heli-skiers/boarders to enjoy themselves.

Range of Trip Durations:

One to seven day tours.

Price Range:

3-Run Daily ($630) to 7-Day Packages ($640)

Operated by the original owner, and maintained as a smaller operation allows us to offer a high standard of client care which creates a more personable experience to our clients. We take pride in and love what we do, and enjoy sharing this experience with our heli-skiing/boarding clients. You should be here!

Canada

Retallack Alpine Adventures Ltd.
PO BOX 147
New Denver, BC
V0G 1S0
Canada
800-330-1433
250-354-5324
www.retallack.com
powder@retallack.com

Price Range: $225 - $600.

"Retallack Alpine Adventures provides cat skiing and snowboarding experiences in the remote mountain wilderness high up in the Selkirk Mountains of BC, Canada, located between the towns of New Denver and Kaslo. It's one of those out-of-the-way places that you'll never forget.

Retallack Resort lodge will be your home base during your powder snow adventures. Expect friendly service and cozy surroundings in our 10,000 square foot mountain lodge. Your meals are carefully prepared by our chef and served in style in our fully licensed dining room. Non-skiers can accompany skiers by special arrangement.

Our season runs from the middle of December until early April. Our booking staff will be pleased to help you decide on a powder ski adventure that is right for your schedule, ability and price range. Bring a group of friends anytime!

Retallack cat skiing and snowboarding is best suited to seasoned powder skiers and boarders. Read more in the terrain and climate and ability levels sections below to decide if we're right for you. Powder snow adventures are a journey, and we want to help you make the most of your steep 'n' deep experience with Retallack.

Retallack prides itself on 'being in the right place'. We have 38 square km. (9500 acres) on three main mountain peaks called Reco, Wishful and Texas. These peaks and their long alpine ridge lines (Reco is 7 km long!) form perfect snowcat access drop off points at elevations between 7000' and 8500'. Our lowest pick-up in the valley floor is at 3000'. Our runs are as long as 3600', so we certainly rival helicopter skiing operations. The average run length is 1800' (600m). The runs are consistent, uninterrupted, fall line skiing.

A simple description of this extremely varied, complicated, compact set of mountains is not possible. But, suffice to say that the two main U-shaped cirques (Stenson and Robb creek drainages) provide runs on all aspects, with the majority of terrain on eastern and western exposures. This allows for the Retallack claim of powder snow until very late in the season

About 20% is moderate/gentle, another 45% is the very FUN steep (between 20 and 35 degrees) and the other 35% is VERY steep (beyond 35 degrees). But, because of the phenomenal snow and consistent fall line, this is fantastic terrain to learn good technique and gain confidence in your powder skiing.

Retallack has approximately 25% open slopes in the form of alpine ridge lines, open bowls, avalanche chutes and large, natural openings in the trees. These features tend to be moderately to extremely steep. The rest of the terrain is treed. We make the distinction in degree by calling it gladed or tree skiing.

The gladed terrain makes for skiing dreams: the snow is protected from the wind and the sun, there is enough elbow room to relax and turn and take spectacular photography. As you descend down the mountain, the trees change from spruce or fir on the upper slopes, to cedar and hemlock old growth forests in the valley bottoms.

You'll think you stepped into a Warren Miller movie. Your friendly guides will give you tips and tricks for skiing efficiently and safely in the land of giants: BC trees!

The discussion of climate is relevant to the snow quality and amount. Due to its sudden sheerness, elevation and geographical location, the Selkirk Range receives moisture laden clouds from the Pacific on a very regular basis that dump dry snow in large amounts. Retallack can receive as much as 100 cm (3.5 ft.) of snow in one storm cycle.

Annually, Retallack receives between 7 and 13 meters (25 - 40 ft) which leaves us with an average base of 3 to 4 meters (10 - 12 ft). The temperatures are more moderate than the Rockies to the east with nighttime lows seldom below -25 deg C, and colder than the Coast with daytime highs staying below freezing, even on northern aspects late into the spring. This allows us to almost guarantee continual powder skiing. Toward the end of March, we can find good powder skiing in the morning and nice spring skiing in the afternoon. It's called the BC Interior... world-renowned snow quality. In combination with the protected slopes that it falls on at Retallack, you can expect VERY GOOD (or better) skiing 100% of the time, and EXCELLENT (to outstanding) skiing 70% of the season," –www.retallack.com.

RK Heliski
PO BOX 695
Invermere, BC
V0A 1K0
Canada
800-661-6060
250-342-3889
www.rkheliski.com
info@rkheliski.com

Range of Trip Durations: 1 – 3 days.

Price Range: $639 - $20,346.

"Our 35 years of experience in the industry means we are experts at what we do and know how to provide an experience over and above our clients' expectations. Rk's staff are renowned for safety being their number one priority. Our staff is professional, conscientious and know they are here to provide our clients with a memorable experience.

Another reason to ski with rk is the exceptional location, rk's site can't be beat. Our proximity to Panorama means that you will never have a day where you cannot ski. There are minimal days that we are unable to access the backcountry due to bad weather, but if you happen to be booked to heli-ski on one of those days, you will not find yourself stranded in the lodge. The opportunity exists for you to ski at Panorama, which is within walking distance from the rklodge.

One of the most important reasons for why you should ski with rk is our guides' field expertise. The first line of defense when working in avalanche terrain is hiring trained professional mountain guides who have appropriate skills and qualifications to work in winter mountain terrain.

Our lead guides are internationally certified as full mountain guides through the UIAGM / IFMGA (International Federation of Mountain Guides Associations), the Association of Canadian Mountain Guides (ACMG) and are professional members of the Canadian Avalanche Association. To meet the exacting standards prescribed by these associations requires years of practical experience and completion of numerous courses and examinations. In order to maintain their professional status, each guide is required to continually maintain and upgrade their skills. Our regular guides are required to be members of the ACMG at the Full Mountain Guide, Ski Guide or Assistant Ski Guide level. As part of their professional qualification, each guide is also required to hold, at minimum, an advanced first aid certification. Some of our guides hold additional qualifications in many other diverse and related fields, including explosive control.

Avalanche professionals describe the three most important things in avalanche safety as terrain, terrain, terrain. This means that selection of the appropriate terrain on any given day is one of the best ways of avoiding avalanche involvements. Trained professional guides have the skills required to make the all important terrain decisions," – www.rkheliski.com.

Robson HeliMagic Inc.
PO BOX 18
Valemount, BC
V0E 2Z0
Canada
877-454-4700
250-566-4700
www.robsonhelimagic.com
brigitta@robsonhelimagic.com

Range of Trip Durations:

Trips are: 1day, 3day, 5day, or 7 day packages

Price Range: $579 - $6,359.

Selkirk Tangiers Heli Skiing
PO BOX 130
Revelstoke, BC
V0E 2S0
Canada
250-837-5378
www.selkirk-tangiers.com
info@selkirk-tangiers.com

Range of Trip Durations:

Trips are: 3day, 5day, 6day, or 7 day packages

Price Range: $2,155 - $7,252.

"Our ski area located in the Interior Mountains of British Columbia can be described as the heart of heli-skiing. We ski in two major mountain ranges, the Monashees to the west and the Selkirks to the east of Revelstoke. Both mountain ranges are noted for reliable powder snow conditions and great terrain. We have established over 200 major runs with countless variations and it is not uncommon to ski new runs.

In marginal and bad weather, the helicopters are prevented access to the open alpine terrain above tree line due to poor visibility, so we will be skiing in the trees. Also, it is safer to ski tree runs during storm cycles due to the increased hazard. Some of the greatest skiing takes place in the forest. The snow is generally superb all the way to the valley floor and normally not affected by the wind.

The world's best tree skiing is to be found in Canada's Columbia Mountains in the interior of B.C. due to specific climatic conditions, species of trees and heavy reliable snowfalls," –www.selkirk-tangiers.com.

Selkirk Wilderness Skiing
1 Meadow Creek Road
Meadow Creek, BC
V0G 1N0
Canada
250-366-4424
www.selkirkwilderness.com
info@selkirkwilderness.com

Range of Trip Durations:

5 days: Monday – Friday. Includes 6 nights accommodation and all meals.

"It isn't about lift lines, crowded runs, or man-made snow. Real skiing & riding is about miles of secluded terrain and deep, dry, powder. It's about the thrill of sharp drops, the exhilaration of snow in your face, and the splendor of majestic mountains. At Selkirk Wilderness Skiing you're sure to ski or ride a total of 12,000 to 18,000 vertical feet each day, all untouched powder, enjoying the more than 400 inches of now that fall on the Selkirks each year.

First time snowcat skiers should be strong intermediates: able to ski and ride the black diamond runs at major lift serviced areas in control, not necessarily with "finesse". They should be reasonably fit and prepared for lots of snowy tumbles. Remember, the landing is soft," – www.selkirkwilderness.com.

Skeena Heliskiing
PO BOX 1032
Smithers, BC
V0J 2N0
Canada
250-877-7811
www.skeenaheliskiing.com
info@skeenaheliskiing.com

Range of Trip Durations:

Trips are: 3day, 4day, or 7 day packages

Price Range: $4,500 - $9,700.

"In the heart of Northern British Columbia lie the Skeena, Atna and Sicintine Mountain Ranges where 8250 km2 of remote wilderness and untouched Canadian powder await. The heliskiing area boasts countless new runs to be explored. This, coupled with breathtaking alpine runs makes Skeena Heliskiing one of Canada's premiere heliskiing areas. Add a 300 to 400+ cm base and you have a skier's nirvana," www.skeenaheliskiing.com.

Snowwater Heli Skiing
PO BOX 1340
Rossland, BC
V0G 1Y0
Canada
866-722-SNOW (7669)
www.snowwater.com
info@snowwater.com

Year Established: 2000

Terrain Description:

Varied terrain with lots of steep and deep mountains in the heart of the Selkirks (8 minute flight from Nelson).

Range of Trip Durations:

Single day, 3 and 5 day trips, and all inclusive packages.

Price Range: $900 – $9,400

Offering snowcat back up with all heli packages (not single day) so you ski every day guaranteed. 12 people max at the lodge to ensure that each client gets lots of personal attention. You are not just a face at Snowwater.

TLH Heliskiing
PO BOX 1118
Vernon, BC
V1T 6N4
800-667-4854
250-558-5379
www.tlhheli.com
info@tlhheli.com

Price Range: From $3,389 for 3 full days.

Tulsequah Heliskiing
PO BOX 2128
Haines Junction, BC
Y0B 1L0
Canada
867-634-2224
www.tqhheliskiing.com
info@tqhheliskiing.com
Price Range: $6,780 - $9,993

"We invite you to come and experience & discover "the Magic and the Mystery" of Tulsequah Heliskiing (TQH). TQH is all about the ultimate heliski & heliboard experience for those individuals who demand the best in Heliskiing & Heliboarding.

TQH specializes in heliskiing & heliboarding in small groups of maximum 10 clients and Private Weeks with 5-10 Skiers & Snowboarders.

Tulsequah Heliskiing`s Location is in pristine Wilderness , close to the border of British Columbia / Canada & Alaska along the Tulsequah River approx. 35 miles north from Juneau - the Capitol of Alaska - which is reached via the International Airport of Seattle. The only access to Tulsequah from Juneau is by Ski-plane or Helicopter.

Our Lodge is a renovated "Historic Gold Mine" with a maximum of 10 clients per week at the Lodge any time. Our Chef will be looking after you with daily fresh pastry, Salad Bar and Gourmet Food throughout the week," --www.tqhheliskiing.com.

Valhalla Powdercats
Nelson, BC
Canada
888-352-7656
www.valhallapow.com
info@valhallapow.com
Price Range: $260 - $400.

Whistler Heli-Skiing
PO BOX 368
Whistler, BC
V0N 1B0
Canada
604-932-4105
www.whistlerheliskiing.com
heliski@direct.ca

Year Established: 1982

Terrain Description:

.5 Million acres, providing over 1,000 runs of high alpine terrain.

Range of Trip Durations:

Single day trips to unlimited days.

Price Range:

$670 per person for 3 Run Classic; $750 per person for 4 Run Elite; $970 per person for 6 Run Ultimate.

Some of the best terrain in all of Canada. You may heli-ski for any number of days and change or cancel a day up to 4pm the day prior to skiing for a full refund. If weather is poor, you can always ski at the world famous Whistler Blackcomb Ski Resort.

$100 discount for second and consecutive days of heli-skiing. Rentals available for $35/day. Video/photography services available. Each group is managed by a professional mountain guide.

White Grizzly Cat Skiing
PO BOX 129
Meadow Creek, BC
V0G 1N0
Canada
250-366-4306
www.whitegrizzly.com
snowcats@direct.ca

Range of Trip Durations: 1 – 6 days.

Price Range: $625 - $3,600

Wildhorse Snowcat Skiing & Powder Mining Co.
306 Victoria Street
Nelson, BC
V1L 4K4
Canada
888-488-4327
www.kootenayexperience.com
catskiing@kootenayexperience.com

Price Range: $285 - $350 per person, per day.

"Perfect Private Powder Skiing daily from Dec 1st - March 30th. Breakfast at the "Palace" in the town of Ymir at 7 a.m. and zip up to Wildhorse Pass as passengers on snowmobiles at 8 a.m. Then it is ski, ski, and ski. Lunch and Drinks Include. We guarantee a minimum of 10,000 vertical feet. This will probably be your best day of skiing ever! Powder Skiing is a great experience to share with your best friends and ski partners. We return to Ymir at around 5PM. Massage Services available at the Ymir Palace. Beer and Food available too." – www.kootenayexperience.com.

9

Europe & Eastern Europe

Every skier has to experience the Alps at some point in their lifetime. The vibe is unique and the skiing is nothing short of phenomenal.

Europeans know how to take après ski activities to a completely different level, with even the most conservative of people finding themselves in compromising situations.

The perfect way to cap off a trip to the Alps is with a day in the heli. The majority of operators are located in Italy, but luckily the locations are convenient from a variety of ski towns.

Go ahead and make this the season that you take the Alps by storm!

Europe & Eastern Europe Operator Directory

France

Chamonix Aventure
Patrick Anulliero
Mountain & Ski Guide
74660 Vallorcine
Chamonix, France
+330680425849
www.chamonix-aventure.com
contact@chamonix-aventure.com
Year Established: 1980

Season: December – May

Terrain Description:

Many possibilities for great off piste skiing, regardless of ski level. Operating in three different locations: Monte Rosa range, Val Veny range, and Switzerland. (France, Italy, Switzerland)

Range of Trip Durations: 1 – 7 days.

Price Range: Starting at $230 Euros/day.

More than 25 years guiding in the Alps. Professional guides are experts on the secret stashes, snow conditions, and safety.

Dream Season

Georgia

Alpin Travel
Seestrasse 60
Postfach 14
8880 Walenstadt
Switzerland
+41 (0)81 720 21 21
www.alpintravel.ch
info@alpintravel.ch
Price Range: 2,600 – 3,150 Euros.

"Welcome to the winter season in Gudauri! The Sporthotel Gudauri and its staff as well as the Heliski team are looking forward to spend with you a great ski week in the Caucasian mountains.

The helicopter will drop you off high up on solitary mountain peaks. The ski enjoyment is incomparable and the "ultimate in skiing": untouched slopes, a marvelous landscape and down in the valleys of the Caucasus there is the helicopter waiting for you to bring you up again for a new enjoyment. A multitude of fantastic downhills between 1500 and 4200 meters of altitude are reached in short approach flights by helicopter from the hotel. An immense ski and snowboard enjoyment waits for you in the Caucasian mountains.

It is our top priority to ensure you safe Heli skiing / snowboarding enjoyment. We try our best to guarantee you an all-round optimal service and an efficient heliski operation," –www.alpintravel.ch.

Italy

Chamonix Aventure
Patrick Anulliero
Mountain & Ski Guide
74660 Vallorcine
Chamonix, France
+330680425849
www.chamonix-aventure.com
contact@chamonix-aventure.com

Year Established: 1980

Season: December – May

Terrain Description:

Many possibilities for great off piste skiing, regardless of ski level. Operating in three different locations: Monte Rosa range, Val Veny range, and Switzerland. (France, Italy, Switzerland)

Range of Trip Durations: 1 – 7 days.

Price Range: Starting at $230 Euros/day.

More than 25 years guiding in the Alps. Professional guides are experts on the secret stashes, snow conditions, and safety.

Heliski Cervinia
+39 0166 949267
Italy
www.heliskicervinia.com
info@heliskicervinia.com

Price Range: 125 - 1,780 Euros.

Dream Season

"Combine the sensation of a helicopter ride with the irresistible allure of a breathtaking off-piste descent on immaculate crystallised snow; all this is possible thanks to heli-skiing, an activity that operates from the 10th January to the 1st May in the Aosta Valley with regional laws that strictly regulate the activity.

Skiing, using a helicopter as a means of reaching the highest points, is without doubt an unforgettable experience, especially in an unspoilt environment encircled by the most beautiful peaks in the Alps. Cervinia is characterised by open spaces and an altitude difference of 1,500 metres in Valtournenche to 4,600 metres of Monte Rosa and represents undoubtedly one of the best destinations for the practice of heli-skiing.

After a snowfall, when the entire valley seems to be still sleeping, there is nothing like a fantastic descent on a slope of untouched powdery snow. A few minutes flight time is all that is needed to reach places of incomparable beauty, where nature reigns; from here you start your descent…from here you start to dream…weightless skis sink softly in the powdery snow and like brushes on a canvas, paint magnificent ribbons, the breeze caressing your face…in the enchanted silence of the deserted wild mountain….the sensation is without comparison.

The practice of heli-skiing is carried out in complete safety and with maximum professionalism: It takes place exclusively with the assistance of an Alpine Guide that, as well as being an excellent skier and expert mountaineer, knows their mountain perfectly and according to the snow conditions, knows the appropriate itineraries to recommend every day. The pilots, with lengthy experience in high altitude flying, will take you soaring between the mountains and glaciers of your dreams,"
www.heliskicervinia.com.

Heliski Valgrisenche
+39 03487121960
Italy
www.heliskivalgrisenche.it
info@heliskivalgrisenche.it

"Valgrisenche is a miniature Canada in the centre of the Alps with 20 drop off points between 3200mt. and 3500mt., a choice of over 100 different descents with a vertical drop of between 1500mt. and 2100mt. Excellent snow conditions, huge open spaces, a real paradise for off piste skiers and snowboarders.

The professionalism of the Alpine Guides and the organization of the Heli base in Canadian style is a guarantee of high quality. Important and distinguished visitors to the Heli base have also helped to create a good image within the valley. The organization offers both to the Guides and its clients a wealth of experience of over 20 years of business.

The person responsible for the Heli base is Danilo Garin, an Alpine Guide from 1981 with extensive experience of Canadian Heliski (C.M.H.) and Kirgikistan. Danilo speaks English, French and Italian."
-- www.heliskivalgrisenche.it.

La Thuile – Funivie Piccolo San Bernardo
Italy
+39 0165 884052
www.lathuile.net
info@lathuile.net

"By helicopter skiers are taken up to the summit of the Rutor glacier (3.486 m.) or the Miravidi glacier (3.051 m.) where an Alpine guide leads the way down through very unique scenery. That is the helicopter experience offered from January 1 to the end of May.

The descent from Rutor glacier joins the Moroir village, France (1220 m.). The lunch time is in a typical Savoyard restaurant. The return to

Piccolo San Bernardo is by French chairlifts. With the Miravidi run, it's possible to arrive till Piccolo San Bernardo and to take lunch in a typical restaurant before to return in La Thuile by slopes. This run is matched with Mont Ouille descent. After the arriving by slopes, helicopter takes people from Piccolo San Bernardo to the top.

Other activities to try are indoor climbing wall, ice falls climbing and nocturnal snowshoe excursions," --www.lathuile.net.

Lyskamm Viaggi
Fraz Centro 44
13021 Alagna Valsesia VC
Italy
www.lyskammviaggi.com
info@lyskammviaggi.com
Price Range: 180 – 230 Euros per person, per day.

"Alagna is still as it has always been, untouched by mass tourism. It offers infinite possibilities for day trips and thanks to the heliski service, which is of course run with all the necessary controls and in compliance with regulatory requirements, more demanding skiers can find fresh winter snow itineraries even in spring. Trust the experience of the Lyskamm Guide, the specialists of Monte Rosa Heliskiing," --www.lyskammviaggi.com.

Monterosa Express
Italy
+46 8 5569 7616
www.monterosa.com
marta@thealps.com
Price Range: $215 - $2,180 Euros.

"We guarantee a lot of skiing, new techniques and tradition. We help you to get there and send you a personal guide for all the time you need.

Call or mail us so we can find out your perfect solution," --www.monterosa.com.

Russia

Yak & Yeti Services
Krasnaya Poliana, Kamtchatka, and Elbruz
47 clos de dessous les reves
7440 Chamonix, France
+33450535367
www.yak-yeti.com
info@yak-yeti.com

Year Established: 1988

Season: December – May

Terrain Description:

Large variety of terrain, satisfying all you interests.

Range of Trip Durations:

3 – 4 days & 7 – 8 days

Price Range:

1,790 to 3,650 Euros

Exotic location with large quantities of deep powder. Experienced worldwide heliski operator since 1980. UIAGM certified Mountain Guides.

Sweden

Totalskidskolan
Hagvagen 17
Strangnas
645 50
SVERIGE
Sweden

+46 0152 122 66
www.totalskidskolan.z.se
bokningen@totalskidskolan.z.se

"If you have been skiing awhile and are now starting to look for more adventure than the average ski area can offer, then enquire about our spring trip to Riksgransen in the North of Sweden. We start off on this excellent ski area for a warm up, then load into the helicopter for the main event. Within minutes we are taken into hidden valleys and peaks that no lift will ever access. International Mountain Guides lead us in a day you'll never forget." --www.totalskidskolan.z.se.

Switzerland

Air Zermatt AG
PO BOX 3920
Zermatt, Switzerland
027 966 86 86
www.air-zermatt.ch
zermatt@air-zermatt.ch

Price Range: 210 – 233 Euros per person, per day.

"Go up by helicopter, come down on skis through pristine powder snow: Heli-skiing is becoming more and more popular," -- www.zermatt.ch.

Chamonix Aventure
Patrick Anulliero
Mountain & Ski Guide
74660 Vallorcine
Chamonix, France
+330680425849
www.chamonix-aventure.com
contact@chamonix-aventure.com
Year Established: 1980

Europe & Eastern Europe

Season: December – May

Terrain Description:

Many possibilities for great off piste skiing, regardless of ski level. Operating in three different locations: Monte Rosa range, Val Veny range, and Switzerland. (France, Italy, Switzerland)

Range of Trip Durations: 1 – 7 days.

Price Range: Starting at $230 Euros/day.

More than 25 years guiding in the Alps. Professional guides are experts on the secret stashes, snow conditions, and safety.

Turkey

Turkey Heliski
CP 155 1936
Verbier, Switzerland
+41 27 771 72 50
www.turkeyheliski.com
info@turkeyheliski.com

Price Range: 5,300 – 11,500 Euros.

10

Greenland

Those not familiar with Greenland will be pleased to know that it is the perfect stopover point between winters in the Northern and Southern Hemispheres. During the months of April to June, it is hard to find better skiing anywhere on earth.

The scenery in Greenland is unique and second to none, with runs lasting from peak to beach! If you think you have the legs for some serious vertical, go to Greenland in May. See how much vertical you can log in a twenty hour stretch as the daylight seems to last forever!

Greenland Operator Directory

Greenland Heliskiing
www.greenlandheliskiing.com

Season: April – May.

Price Range: 8,900 Euros.

"Come ski the wild terrain of West Greenland with 2000 meter runs to the water's edge in deep powder and corn snow, make the Greenlandic experience life's best. Based 60 kilometers north of Maniitsoq, in the tiny village of Kangaamiut, we live close to the local population and their daily routine. We rent houses from a few of the families, and gather together in the evening for our home cooked meal," – www.greenlandheliskiing.com.

Heliski Greenland
BP 82
73152 Val D'isere Cedex
Greeenland
+33 6 11 32 71 72
www.heliskigreenland.com
heliskigreenland@yahoo.fr

Year Established: 2000

Season: April 20 – June 3

Terrain Description:

75% glacier runs, large runs, steep couloirs, stunning views, combination of both challenging and easy runs.

Range of Trip Durations: 6 – 8 days.

Price Range: ~8,300 Euros per person.

Dream Season

Most runs end on the beach, with stunning 360 degree views. Heli and boat transfer used daily. 4 guests & 1 guide per group, 3 groups maximum per week. New runs (first descents) almost every week. Elevation change of 1800 meters to sea level makes for easy breathing and wind protection. Powder and corn can be had on the same run.

This is one of the most unknown locations in the world, including fantastic scenery of the ice-caps and the sea. These are the longest heliskiing days you can find anywhere. In the middle of May, daylight stretches from 3 AM to 11 PM.

11

Himalayas

The Himalayas are the Superbowl of heli-skiing and every other mountain sport. Traveling to the Himalayas will cost you a pretty penny, but is sure to be the experience of a lifetime.

One of the major distinguishing factors about the Himalayas is the amount of vertical that can be obtained. Runs are high quality, very long, and offer everything from alpine views to amazing glade runs including birch, oak, and cedar forests.

This is your chance to ski literally at the top of the world, with views of all of the famous peaks, including Everest!

Dream Season

Himalaya Operator Directory

Himichal Helicopter Skiing
PO BOX 1000
2633 Dunsmuir Ave.
Cumberland, BC
V0R 1S0
Canada
250-336-2501
www.himachal.com
himachal@shaw.ca

Price Range: 6,000 – 7,500+ Euros.

"The powder skiing at Manali is exceptional! Our location at approximately 34° N. latitude, roughly equivalent to Los Angeles, gives us long days, and a variety of exposures allows us to ski both with or against the sun. The altitude allows much greater "back radiation" than other areas, which creates excellent recrystallised powder. Manali is known for having one of the deepest snowpacks in the entire Himalaya, and due to our continental climate, snowfalls tend to be of low moisture content. As an added bonus, the potential is vast for terrific, spring corn-snow skiing!

With regard to your transportation to New Delhi, Indira Gandhi International Airport / New Delhi is serviced by most major international carriers who provide comfortable and convenient options. Please note that HHS leaves all international transportation responsibilities with the guest! We recommend that you book your travel plans early as flights in and out of New Delhi tend to be quite busy. Be sure that you are able to make all connections and itineraries, as failure to do so could delay your arrival in Manali.

The altitudes at which we ski vary depending on group fitness and ability, the interests of the group and the snow and weather conditions. HHS has wonderful conditions at the same elevations as resorts in America and Europe, but the opportunity exists to ski on what is truly the roof of the world. Most skiing takes place between high valley floors around two thousand, seven hundred meters and ridges at four thousand, three hundred meters, with vertical averaging between nine hundred meters and twelve hundred meters. However, some of our most spectacular terrain is as high as five thousand meters. Please note that we do not require anyone to ski at these altitudes and our guides reserve the right to deny access to these higher altitude runs to anyone for any reason whatsoever," –www.himachal.com.

Himalayan Heliski Guides
Residence Brevent, Bat. "A"
37 Chemin des Bios
74400 Chamonix, France
+33 (0)6 27 69 38 02
www.heliskinepal.com
info@heliskinepal.com

Year Established: 2002

Season: February - April

Terrain Description:

Ski the Everest & Annapurna regions of Nepal. Every type of terrain is available, from low angle to steep; big open bowls to couloirs, etc.

Range of Trip Durations:

Saturday to Sunday (6 days skiing).

Price Range: $6,500 (US Dollars) and up.

The first and only heliski company in Nepal's Himalaya. This is adventure skiing at its best, and a Nepal experience all at the same time.

Heliskiing in Nepal is for the person who wants adventure in life as well as to take part in the history of opening up Nepal's Himalaya to skiing. Skiing in the Annapurna and Everest regions is simply beyond words, it is a dream come true. When you add the culture side of a heliski trip in Nepal, you have a very unique experience, which will stay with you as one of the best ski trips and experiences in your life.

Himalaya Heliski Kashmir
Saudan's Club
BP 2076
CH-1211 Geneve 1
www.himalaya-heliski-cachemire.com
himalaya.heliski@sylvain-saudan.com

Price Range: 6,950 – 8,450 Euros.

"Deep down in every skier's subconscious is the desire, once in a lifetime, to make tracks in virgin snow on the most mythical mountains on earth, where the abominable snowman is more than a legend.

Honorary Citizen of Kashmir (first skier to descend a 23,000 feet summit, the highest peak of Kashmir: Nun-Kun), used to its mountains and its snow, Sylvain Saudan selected Srinagar to set Himalaya Heliski base, with a skiing area equivalent to the Northern and Southern Alps brought together.

Sylvain Saudan's distinguished reputation as a man of exploits, his entry in the Guinness Book of Records for his vertiginous ski descents in the Alps and in the Himalayas, often overshadows his real personality: a man of prudence and of measure, an expert on snow, a ski technician who has taught skiing on all five continents," – www.himalaya-heliski-cachemire.com.

Kashmir Powdercats
Gulmarg, Kashmir, India
612 99222557 (April to November)
www.skihimalaya.com
peter@skihimalaya.com

Year Established: 2005

Kashmir Powdercats guiding services commenced operations in winter 2005/2006. The first season saw 60 visitors from 10 countries, resulting in the employment of 8 local Kashmiri guides and drivers. Commercial snow-cat skiing operations will commence in winter 2007/2008 following trial operations in winter 2006/2007.

12

New Zealand

New Zealand has become one of the hottest destinations for heli-skiing during the months of July – October. Most of the heli-skiing industry in New Zealand is centered around the Queenstown area on South Island. This area offers affordable rates, great powder, and breathtaking sights.

In order to supplement your heli trip with other activities, you can plan a stop in Australia or take part in the many excursions offered on South Island. These excursions include: resort skiing, heli-tours, heli-hiking, paragliding, surfing, bungee jumping, national parks, fiords, whale and penguin watching, etc.

The opportunities in New Zealand are limitless as this is the ultimate destination for adventure seekers.

Dream Season

NEW ZEALAND

New Zealand Operator Directory

Alpine Heliski
34 Shotover Street
Queenstown, New Zealand
03 441 2300
www.alpineheliski.com
ski@alpineheliski.com

Year Established: 2005

Season: June 15 – October 15 (depending on snow)

Terrain Description:

Queenstown: Eyre, Hector, and Richardson Mountains.
Wanaka: Minaret Ranges.

Range of Trip Durations:

Day packages ranging from 3 – 8 runs.
Day and multi-day private charter options.

Price Range:

3 run: $649, 4 run: $739, 6 run: $869, 8 run: $1029
Private charter: $5,995 per day (up to five people)

In establishing our new company, we've taken the experience we've had from working for other operations, and made every single thing 10% better. From our team of experienced guides, to our top-notch exclusive terrain, to the vans we drive people in, to the lunches we provide…it all adds up to give the best quality heliski experience available.

"At Alpine Heli-Ski Ltd we are driven by a passion for deep snow, maximum freedom and chasing the ultimate alpine adventure. Our backyard is the Southern Alps of New Zealand – both beautiful and wild. Let us turn your Heli-Ski dream into reality!

Alpine Heli-Ski Ltd is a highly professional and dynamic Heli-Ski/Boarding operation. We provide outstanding day, multi-day, and private charter Heli-Ski/Boarding on spectacular untouched alpine terrain surrounding the world-renowned adventure travel destinations of Queenstown and Wanaka.

Our team has decades of local and international experience between them – not just in Heli-Ski guiding, but in all aspects of alpine mountaineering."

Backcountry Helicopters
103 Ardmore Street
Wanaka
New Zealand
+64 3 443 1059
www.heliskinz.com
info@heliskinz.com

Price Range: $660 – $880 per person, per day.

"The pinnacle of ski experiences is a clear day, fresh snow and the most unbelievable terrain to explore. Heliskiing with BCH is the experience to surpass all others. We give you pure freedom in terrain that you could only dream existed. There are no lift lines, no long lift rides, no crowds, just your group, guide and a helicopter waiting to take you on your adventure.

BCH use only the best guides and understand modern free skiing requirements. Our guides are there to make every run the best of your life. We search out the best conditions of the day. We pick out the terrain that best suits your ability. This may mean we start off in open bowls and faces but maybe finding something more challenging by the afternoon. We are as flexible as possible while always keeping safety in mind.

Mt Aspiring National Park is fast becoming the choice of the best skiers in the world. Its varying terrain lends itself well to heliskiing. Giving many options from open bowls and valleys to steep chutes and faces we have something for all abilities. For intermediate skiers we have many options where we can take you away from the crowded ski resorts into tranquility with awesome views of both Lake Wanaka and Lake Hawea," --www.heliskinz.com.

Christchurch Helicopters
PO BOX 36-450
Christchurch
New Zealand
800-HELOTEK
www.heliskitekapo.co.nz
enquiries@heliskitekapo.co.nz

Price Range: $310 - $1310 per person, per day.

"Experience heli skiing/boarding at its best. Ski/board in the Two Thumb, Hazard Ranges, and on the Tasman Glacier. We offer runs of intermediate through to expert. Long open bowl skiing/boarding through to steep and deep. Long runs, usually between 2,500-3,500 vertical feet, mean you spend more time on the snow.

We offer one run heli lifts through to seven day adventure packages. Report to our 'Heli Hut', (Saturday/Sunday - all other days require booking), at Roundhill Ski Area if you are wanting to experience one or two heli lifts. However, bookings are essential for the more adventurous Heliski/boarding packages.

Heliskiing/boarding takes us to high altitudes. Therefore you can experience powder and corn skiing in the same day. Weather in the New Zealand Alps is very changeable due to our maritime climate. Statistically we ski/board around four out of seven days. So, make sure to allow suitable time frames to ensure some great skiing/boarding." --www.heliskitekapo.co.nz.

Harris Mountains Heli-Ski
The Station, Cnr Shotover & Camp Sts
PO BOX 634
Queenstown
New Zealand
+64 3 442 6722
www.heliski.co.nz
hmh@heliski.co.nz

Price Range: $725 - $1275 per person, per day.

"Way back in the late seventies and early eighties, heli-skiing was developed in New Zealand.

From these early days evolved Harris Mountains Heli-ski, our locally owned and operated company operating in the Southern Alps, Harris Mountains and beyond.

Over 26 years in operation and being the largest heli-ski company in New Zealand has meant we have discovered the best heli-ski terrain available for heli-skiers and boarders to enjoy. We are a professional and dynamic Heli-Ski/Boarding operation and with years of experience we are able to offer a highly sophisticated safety infrastructure. We provide outstanding daily, multi-day and private charters heli-ski/boarding on our exclusive and expansive variety of terrain," – www.heliski.co.nz.

Heli Ski Queenstown
PO BOX 2094
Queenstown
New Zealand
+64 3 442 7733
www.flynz.co.nz
bookings@flynz.co.nz

Price Range: $745 - $1,800 per person, per day.

"Heli Guides has over 50,000 hectares of heli skiing and boarding country to choose from. Exclusive access to these areas enables runs of 2,000 - 4,000 foot vertical from intermediate through to the steep and challenging. Our Chief Guide and snow safety officers carefully select the terrain we utilize on the day after consideration of weather patterns, snow conditions and client skiing ability," --www.flynz.co.nz.

Methven Heliskiing
Arrowsmith Range
Methven, South Island
New Zealand
+64 3 302 8108
www.heliskiing.co.nz
methven@heliskiing.co.nz

Price: $795 – standard day, per person.

"Methven Heliskiing - an awesome heliskiing and heliboarding experience among New Zealand's biggest range of terrain.

Unique to New Zealand, helipad is based at Glenfalloch, a high-country sheep station. On the 50 minute scenic drive from Methven the only traffic jams you may experience will be flocks of Merino sheep!

Within 10 minutes flying time you are amongst it... Unreal scenery and out of this world terrain." –www.heliskiing.co.nz.

Mt. Potts Backcountry
Hakatere Potts Road
Canterbury, New Zealand
0800 SNOWCAT (within NZ)
+64 3 303 9060 (outside NZ)
www.mtpotts.co.nz
info@mtpotts.co.nz

Price Range: $350 - $785.

"Dubbed the new Spot X by a visiting La Grave guide, Mt. Potts is New Zealand's only heli accessed snowcat skiing experience. Join a group of no more than fourteen guests skiing the steeps, powder, chutes and basins of Mt. Potts. Mt. Potts is the highest ski area in the South Island and captures most of its snow from the reliable Nor'West. Mt. Potts is only one hour's drive from Methven." – www.mtpotts.co.nz.

Ski The Tasman
Tasman Glacier
Aoraki/Mount Cook Region
South Island, New Zealand
+64 3 435 1834
www.skithetasman.co.nz
mtcook@alpineguides.co.nz

Price: $685 per person per day.

"For more than 40 years Ski The Tasman has been New Zealand's classic skiing adventure. This is an extraordinary skiing day into the heart of New Zealand's Southern Alps, in Mt Cook National Park.

Every fine day small groups of adventurous skiers are brought to the white vastness of the Tasman, New Zealand's longest glacier (27 km).

Throughout the day, side trips to explore ice caves and seracs - amazing ice features sculpted by the elements - make the journey unforgettable," –www.skithetasman.co.nz.

Southern Lakes Heliski
PO BOX 426
Queenstown
New Zealand
+64 3 442 6222
www.southernlakesheliski.co.nz
info@southernlakesheliski.co.nz

Price Range: $560 - $880 per person, per day.

"Specializing in exclusive groups and daily group skiing. We provide excellent personalized service with a wide variety of options to choose from.

When you ski with Southern Lakes Heliski you ski or ride with the best team of guides and pilots in New Zealand. Each season our personnel take great pride in providing the best overall heliskiing/heliboarding trip by focusing on our guests' safety and enjoyment. Southern Lakes Heliski skis or rides with one guide and a maximum of 5 guests. We are totally flexible. This is your dream day during your ski holiday in Queenstown and Wanaka. Choose the options that suit you best. From Glaciers to gentle or steep, beginner or expert, it is up to you. Endless mountains or pristine, untouched terrain is all waiting for you," –www.southernlakesheliski.co.nz.

Wilderness Heliskiing
Aoraki/Mount Cook Region
South Island, New Zealand
+64 3 435 1834
www.heliskiing.co.nz
mtcook@heliskiing.co.nz

Price: $795 – standard day, per person.

"Wilderness Heliskiing is about thousands of meters of untracked, unspoiled riding and skiing - set against the panorama of New Zealand's highest peaks. This is the real wilderness experience!

Based at Aoraki/Mount Cook, Wilderness Heliskiing gets you amongst the highest peaks in the country. Expect big vertical, dramatic peaks, and pristine terrain. Classic heliskiing at its best."
–www.heliskiing.co.nz.

13

South America

Every powder addict has dreamed of spending time in the Andes. This is the type of trip that will be burned into your memory for ages. The terrain is top notch, with steeps to challenge even the best of skiers, and the snow is deep and fluffy! The snow usually falls in short, intense storms followed by many days of blue skies, resulting in very few down days.

When you combine the excellent skiing, timing of the season (June – October), and the unique local culture of South America, you'll have an amazing experience to hold onto for the rest of your life.

South America Operator Directory

Andes Heliski
233 Providencia
Santiago, Chile
562-810-4800
www.andesheliski.cl
info@andesheliski.cl

Price Range: $6,845 USD

"Heliski started in Chile in 1987, when a small group of friends gathered together and decided to explore the majestic and beloved Andes mountain range. Little by little we discovered a wonderful treasure, which through the years, and with the incorporation of new friends and mountain lovers, who were in activity for 11 years, we decided to found Andes Heliski, the first heliski/heliboarding company in Chile.

The homologation of the vast territory, that we use exclusively, and the professionalism and preparation of each one of us makes of Andes Heliski a reference point for anyone wanting to live an unforgettable experience.

It is well known that the snow and the climate of the central Chilean mountain range have unique virtues on the world. We challenge you to join us in a new and wonderful experience, one you never lived before." –www.andesheliski.cl.

Dream Season

Andes Ski Tours
1387 Esteban Adrogue St.
2nd Floor, Suite 20
B1846FHG
Buenos Aires, Argentina
866-265-1906
www.andesskitours.com
info@andesskitours.com

Powder South Heliski Guides
1303 Sumac Avenue
Boulder, CO 80304
USA
303-447-2858
888-203-9354
www.heliskiguides.com
powder@heliskiguides.com

Established: 3 years.

Season: June – October.

Range of Trip Durations: 3 days to 1 week.

Price Range: $1,500 to $7,880 USD.

Pioneering a new level of heli skiing in the rugged and beautiful Andes mountain range. Heli ski packages offering thousands of vertical feet of untouched champagne powder in the most alluring and pristine terrain the Andes has to offer during June through October, the Southern Hemisphere's winter season. All guides are UIAGM Certified.

14

Western United States

The Western United States provides an excellent introduction to heli-skiing as well as challenge to accomplished skiers. There are many opportunities to get your feet wet with day trips operating out of most major ski towns. This provides an excellent introduction without committing the time or money to a major multi-day package. Down days can largely be eliminated in these types of situations as you can ski the local resorts in the event that you can't fly on a given day.

There are many opportunities for competent heli-skiers to challenge themselves on some very exciting terrain. This is the best way to ski the resorts you love, while getting a chance to explore outside the resort boundaries in style. These operators make it easy to add a day in the heli to the family vacation you have planned!

Powder Tours
in Beautiful Northeastern Oregon

2,000 acres of steeps, bowls, and glades with up to 1,500 vertical feet per run

- **Half Day**: 3 – 5 runs (w/lift ticket) & snacks
- **Full Day**: up to 10 runs, includes lunch

Highest base elevation in Oregon: 7,100 ft.

541.856.3277
North Powder, OR

AnthonyLakes.com

Western United States Operator Directory

California

Pacific Crest Snowcats
3037 River Road at Squaw Valley
Tahoe City, CA 96145
USA
888-Swayback
530-581-1767
www.pacificcrestsnowcats.com
info@swayback.com

Year Established: 2001

Terrain Description:

Open slopes, tree runs, steep facing chutes, and North facing bowls.

Range of Trip Durations: Day & Multi-Day.

Price Range: $275 per person per day.

Colorado

Chicago Ridge Snowcat Tours
PO BOX 896
Leadville, CO 80461
USA
719-486-2277
www.skicooper.com
chicagoridge@skicooper.com

Price Range: $250 per person, per day.

"Join us on the Chicago Ridge Snowcat Tours and experience the adventure and excitement of backcountry powder skiing and snowboarding. We have over 2400 acres of treed slopes and open bowls, terrain suitable for the advanced to expert skiers/riders. We will take you as high as 12,600 feet in elevation atop the Continental Divide. The slopes vary from 3000 to 10,000 feet in length with vertical drops up to 1400 feet per run. Check in is at the Ski Cooper day lodge. Please bring appropriate gear for snow and changing weather conditions. This is a great opportunity to rent powder fat skies from our rental shop," –www.skicooper.com.

El Diablo Snowcat Skiing
Molas Pass, CO
USA
877-241-9643
www.snowcat-powder.com
info@snowcat-powder.com

Price Range: $220 per person, per day.

"The San Juan Mountains of southwest Colorado provide the spectacular landscape for the awesome adventures of El Diablo Alpine Guides. In 1879 a huge fire burned the upper reaches of Lime Creek leaving us with an open expanse of treeless terrain and beautiful glades, perfectly suited to efficient cat skiing. Most runs begin above timberline and are peppered with steep shots, rock outcroppings, cornices and cliffbands, providing the opportunity for exciting airtime and epic powder turns. We offer special days in the mountains, shared with a group of friends who seek the uncommon experience," --www.snowcat-powder.com.

Monarch Snowcat Tours
Monarch Mountain
23715 W. Hwt. 50
Monarch, CO 81227
USA
888-996-7669 ext. 5199
www.skimonarch.com
snowcat@skimonarch.com

Season: January – April.

Price Range:

$150 - $200 per person per day.
$1,350 – $2,000 Full Cat (12 people) per day.

San Juan Ski Company
Snowcat Skiing
1831 Lake Purgatory Dr.
Durango, CO 81301
USA
800-208-1780
www.sanjuanski.com
powder@sanjuanski.com

Price Range: $200 - $220 per person, per day.

Steamboat Powdercats
1724 Mount Werner Circle
Steamboat Springs, CO 80487
USA
800-288-0543
www.steamboatpowdercats.com
adventures@blueskywest.com

Price Range: $259 - $359 per person, per day.

Telluride Helitrax
300 W. Colorado
Suite B-2
Box 1560
Telluride, CO 81435
USA
866-Heli-Ski (866-435-4754)
970-728-8377
www.helitrax.net
powder@helitrax.net

Year Established: 1982

Season: Mid-January thru Mid-April

Dream Season

Terrain Description:

San Juan Mountains. Greatest concentration of 13,000 and 14,000 summits south of the Yukon. Mostly high alpine powder skiing with man couloirs.

Range of Trip Durations:

Single-Day to Multi-Day

Price Range:

$895 Single Day Heliski
$1,095 per day heliskiing, lodging, meals

Our high elevation (10,500 to 13,700 feet) allows for cold powder skiing all winter long and into the spring when other areas have melted out or turned to slush.

Skier safety and snow quality are our top priorities.

Vail Snowcat Skiing
2328 Garmisch Dr. Ste B
Vail, CO 81657
USA

Idaho

Brundage Snow Cat Skiing & Boarding
PO BOX 1062
McCall, ID 83638
USA
888-ALL-SNOW
208-634-SNOW
www.brundage.com
info@brundage.com

Price Range: $115 - $235 per person, per day.

"Experience the thrill of the backcountry. Join us on a guided Cat trip into the backcountry of the Payette National Forest. Brundage Mountain's experienced guides - licensed by the Idaho Outfitters and Guides Association - will see to it that your adventure into this pristine, snowy wonderland is safe and unforgettable. Snow cat trips for the adventurous are offered on over 19,000 acres of snowy steeps and powdery bowls. Brundage Mountain's Cat adventures are hosted by experienced backcountry guides. Skiers and Snowboarders welcome on our trips," –www.brundage.com.

Peak Adventures Snowcat Skiing
PO BOX 50
36112 Canyon Rd.
Cataldo, ID 83810
USA
208-682-3200
www.peaksnowcats.com
terri@peaksnowcats.com

Season: December – April.

Price Range: $250 - $1,500.

Only 60 freeway miles east of the Spokane Washington airport, headquarters are easy to access and convenient for people who don't want to spend their vacation driving on winter roads or crossing international borders.

Selkirk Powder Company
Schweitzer Mountain Resort
Sandpoint, Idaho
USA
866-GO IDAHO
208-263-6959
www.selkirkpowderco.com
info01@selkirkpowderco.com

Price Range: $250 - $2,300.

Sun Valley Heli Ski Guides, Inc.
PO BOX 978
Sun Valley, ID 83353
USA
800-872-3108
208-622-3108
www.svheli-ski.com
info@sunvalleyheliski.com
Price Range: $550 - $7,800.

"It is only fitting that the birthplace of heli-skiing in the United States is Sun Valley, Idaho—the same locale dubbed "America's First Destination Ski Resort."

The mountains surrounding the town of Ketchum were discovered in 1935 to be the ideal surroundings for a ski resort and the opening of the Sun Valley Resort followed just one year later. The same spectacular terrain and pioneering spirit of the region led to the founding of Sun Valley Heli-Ski Guides in 1966 by Bill Janss, the owner of Sun Valley Resort.

As the company has witnessed changes in ownership, progression to quieter and more powerful aircraft, and the general evolution of the sport of skiing. The company's tradition of untracked powder, exploration, and adventure remains with each present-day heli-ski trip. As SVHSG celebrates 20 years of ownership by Mark Baumgardner, we are excited to watch heli-skiing in the Sun Valley area continue into the twenty-first century," --www.svheli-ski.com.

Montana

Big Mountain Snowcat Adventures
PO BOX 1400
Whitefish, MT 59937
USA
406-862-2900
www.bigmtn.com
info@bigmtn.com

Price Range: Lift Ticket + $100 per person, per day.

"With the popularity of out-of bounds skiing growing each winter, Big Mountain invites you to an introduction to the backcountry. Come experience the thrill of skiing uncut powder snow on gentle, gladed slopes. We access the powder fields from "Flower Point" where our snow cat will drop you for the run of your life. After wiping the snow off your goggles, we'll take a lift on the Big Creek Express high-speed quad, then ski back to meet our cat driver for another lift. Groups generally ski 5-8 runs per day, and cost is $100/person in addition to a lift ticket. It's an affordable – and fun way to experience what you see in the ski movies," –www.bigmtn.com.

Montana Backcountry Adventures
PO BOX 160815
Big Sky, MT 59716
USA
406-995-3880
www.skimba.com

Nevada

Ruby Mountain Helicopterskiing
PO BOX 28-1192
Lamoille, NV 89828
USA
775-753-6867
www.helicopterskiing.com
info@helicopterskiing.com

Year Established: 1977

Season: January – April.

Terrain Description:

Located in the Ruby Mountains of Eastern Nevada. This region of the Rocky Mountains is known for its dry snow.

Range of Trip Duration: 3 day trips.

Price Range: $3,300

Oregon

Cat Ski Mt Bailey
c/o Diamond Lake Resort
350 Resort Drive
Diamond Lake, Oregon 97731
USA
800-733-7593 ext. SKI
www.catskimtbailey.com
catski@diamondlake.net

Price Range: $250 per person, per day.

Ski Anthony Lakes
Catskiing
47500 Anthony Lake Highway
North Powder, OR 97867
USA
541-856-3277 ext. 12
www.anthonylakes.com
ski@anthonylakes.com

Price Range: $85 - $160.

Utah

Diamond Peaks Heli Ski Adventures
PO BOX 450
Eden, UT 84310
USA
801-745-4631
www.diamondpeaks.com
heli-ski@diamondpeaks.com

Price Range: $625.

Park City Powder Cats & Heli-Ski
PO BOX 681807
Park City, UT 84068
USA
435-649-6596
www.pccats.com
pccat@xmission.com

"Welcome to our world of some of the best powder skiing and snowboarding in North America. Park City Powder Cats and Heli-Ski has been guiding thousands of skiers and riders to untracked terrain in the majestic Unita Mountains since 1992.

Make this the season you experience unbelievable powder skiing with us on over 40,000 acres, privately owned by Thousand Peaks Ranch. Let one of our knowledgeable guides take you on the backcountry trip of a lifetime. Whether you choose riding in one of our two custom heated snow cats or flying high to try some of our more challenging terrain by helicopter, we will make your powder skiing trip a memorable one," --www.pccats.com.

Powder Mountain Winter Resort
Lightning Ridge Snowcat Skiing
PO BOX 450
Eden, UT
USA
801-745-3771
www.powdermountain.com
powdermountain@powdermountain.com

Price Range: $7 per single ride pass.

"One of Powder Mountain's greatest assets, the Lighting Ridge Snowcat will tow you to the top of Lightning Ridge with very little effort. Once on top you will access over 700 challenging acres of pristine powder snow with an impressive 2100' vertical drop.

Access to James Peak and the adjacent powder bowls and chutes are an additional 20-30 minute hike from the top of Lightning Ridge,"
--www.powdermountain.com.

Wasatch Powderbird Guides
PO BOX 920057
Snowbird, UT 84092
USA
800-742-2800
801-974-4354
www.powderbird.com
info@powderbird.com

Price Range: $665 - $840.

Washington

Cascade Powder Cats 2
13410 NE 175th St.
Woodinville, WA 98072
USA
877-SKI-CATS
www.cascadepowdercats.com
info@cascadepowdercats.com

Price Range: $395 per person, per day.

"Skiers and snowboarders who love adventure and luxury take heed! Now you can Escape to the Backcountry with Cascade Powder Cats 2. Located on Stevens Pass, just north of Seattle, CPC2 is the ultimate snow skiing experience in the Northwest. We offer you the chance to rip it up on a minimum of 10,000 vertical feet a day (6-15 runs, depending on which slopes are accessed). We'll transport you in one of our 10 person, fully enclosed (and heated) Snow Cats. Enjoy spectacular views of the Cascade Mountains while you take advantage of untracked POWDER all day long! We also provide beverages, snacks, and a gourmet lunch to complete the experience,"
--www.cascadepowdercats.com.

WESTERN UNITED STATES

North Cascade Heli-Skiing
PO BOX 367
Winthrop, WA 98862
USA
800-494-HELI
509-996-3272
www.heli-ski.com
info@heli-ski.com

Price Range: $800 - $4,860.

"The North Cascades of Washington state, also known as "The American Alps," are the most glaciated peaks in the continental U.S. Our location in the northeast corner of this range is a unique combination of longitude, latitude and altitude, giving us some of the finest snow conditions available anywhere.

Founded in 1988, North Cascade Helicopter Skiing is based out of the Freestone Inn in the Methow Valley. Within our 300,000-acre permit area on the Okanogan National Forest, we can access a vast variety of runs starting at altitudes of 7,500 to 9,000 feet and offering 1,500 to 4,000 vertical-foot drops," --www.heli-ski.com.

Wyoming

Grand Targhee Resort
SnowCat Adventures
PO BOX SKI
Alta, WY 83414
USA
800-TARGHEE
307-353-2300
www.grandtarghee.com
info@grandtarghee.com

Price Range: $299 per person, per day.

"One of the hallmarks of the Grand Targhee experience is a SnowCat adventure on Peaked Mountain. For you and just nine other skiers/riders, a huge powder reserve of 1,000 acres awaits and up to 20,000 vertical feet in a day. Come follow our expert guides through expansive north-facing bowls, mellow, gladed cruisers and steep treed pitches, with breathtaking views of the Tetons all around – one of the greatest thrills in North America," --www.grandtarghee.com.

High Mountain Heli-Skiing
PO BOX 173
Teton Village, WY 83025
USA
307-733-3274
www.heliskijackson.com
heli-ski@wyoming.com

Year Established: 1974

Season: December 18 – April 10

Terrain Description:
Vast open bowls, steep chutes, enchanted glades and forests can all be yours to explore with High Mountain Heli-Skiing.

Range of Trip Durations:
Daily trip includes 6 runs, approximately 12,000 to 15,000 total vertical feet and includes a deli lunch.

Price Range:
$725/day per person, extra runs $75, packages available.

We fly the Bell 407 which allows us small intimate groups (1:5 guide ratio). If we are unable to fly, due to weather, you have the world renowned Jackson Hole Mountain Resort to insure you'll be skiing every day.

Untracked, Untouched, Unbelievable. Since 1974, High Mountain Heli-Skiing has been serving up some of the best powder skiing in North America. Let the guides with over 30 years of experience show you the adventure.

Index

A

Air Zermatt AG, 90
Alaska Backcountry Adventures, 36
Alaska Heliskiing, 36
Alaska Rendezvous Heli Guides, 37
Alberta, 56, 62
Alcoholic beverages, 4
Alpin Travel, 84
Alpine, 8, 21, 22, 23, 24, 25, 30, 43, 53, 58, 62, 63, 64, 65, 72, 76, 77, 80, 95, 103, 104, 118
Alpine Heliski, 6, 9, 10, 11, 12, 13, 14, 15, 103
Alps, 21, 82, 83, 85, 86, 87, 91, 98, 105, 125
Alta, 125
Americans, 22
Anchorage, 29, 31, 32
Andes, 110, 111, 112
Andes Heliski, 111
Andes Ski Tours, 112
Annapurna, 97, 98
Anthony, Chris, 1, 3, 35, 50
Aoraki, 108, 109
Aosta Valley, 86
Après ski, 82
Argentina, 112
Armstrong, Rick, 33
Arrowsmith Range, 107
A-Star, 40, 49, 62, 68
Atlin, 61
Australia, 100
Avalanche, 5, 8, 55, 72, 74

B

Backcountry Helicopters, 104
Baldface Lodge Snowcat Skiing, 53
Banff, 56
BC, 20, 24, 49, 53, 54, 56, 57, 58, 59, 60, 61, 62, 63, 64, 65, 66, 67, 69, 70, 71, 72, 73, 75, 76, 77, 78, 79, 80, 81, 96
Beach, 92, 94
Beer, 6
Bell Helicopter, 1
Bella Coola, 53, 57, 66
Bella Coola Heli Sports, 53
Big Mountain Snowcat Adventures, 120
Big Red Cats, 54
Big Sky, 121
Bixby, Bill, 33
Black, Micah, 30
Blackcomb Helicopters, 54
Blomidon Cat Skiing, 55
Blue River, 2, 49, 63
Bluebird, 4, 41, 44, 67
Boulder, 112
Bowls, 7, 8, 20, 53, 69, 72, 97, 104, 105, 115, 119, 124, 126
British Columbia, 2, 44, 49, 57, 59, 63, 66, 67, 68, 75, 77, 79
Brookbank, Wendy, 33
Brundage Snow Cat Skiing & Boarding, 118
Buenos Aires, 112
Bugaboos, 20

C

California, 115

Canada, vii, 2, 20, 22, 40, 43, 49, 53, 54, 55, 56, 57, 58, 59, 60, 61, 62, 63, 64, 65, 66, 67, 69, 71, 73, 75, 76, 77, 78, 79, 80, 81, 87, 96
Canadian Mountain Holidays, 56
Canadian Rockies, 20, 21
Canterbury, 107
Cariboos, 20
Cascade Powder Cats 2, 124
Cat, 25, 26, 64, 71, 116, 119, 121
Cat Powder Skiing, 56
Cat Ski Mt. Bailey, 122
Cataldo, 119
Caucasian Mountains, 84
Centerfold, 21
Cervinia, 86
Chairlift, 20, 25
Chamonix, 83, 85, 89, 90, 97
Chamonix Aventure, 83, 85, 90
Chase, 64
Chatter Creek Cat & Heli Skiing, 56
Chet Simmons, 34
Chicago Ridge Snowcat Tours, 115
Chile, 111
Christchurch, 105
Christchurch Helicopters, 105
Chugach, 1, 20, 22, 24, 29, 30, 31, 34, 35, 36, 37, 38, 39, 41, 42
Chugach Powder Guides, 31, 38
Chutes, 26, 72, 105, 108, 115, 124, 126
Clothing, 5
Coast Mountains, 57, 67
Coast Range, 20, 24, 57
Coast Range Heliskiing, 57
Coffey, Frank, 2, 31
Coldstream, 63
Colorado, 23, 25, 26, 115, 116, 117
Columbia River, 20, 21
Continental Divide, 25, 116
Conway, Dean, 2, 33
Conway, Jim, 33
Coombs, Doug, 2, 33
Cordova, 2, 29, 30, 32, 39
Corner Brook, 55
Cornice, 26
Cosmic nightclub, 16, 17
Costas, Bob, 22
Cozad, Mike, 2, 33
Crawford, Patrick, 24, 27
Crescent Spur, 57
Crescent Spur Helicopter Holidays, 57

Cummings, Dean, 2, 34

D

Davenport, Chris, 33
Deep Purgation, 16
Deslaurier, 33
Diamond Lake, 122
Diamond Lake Resort, 122
Diamond Peaks Heli Ski Adventures, 122
Dog Heaven, 26
Dog Leg, 26
Dog, Sean, 2
Dogs Run Free, 26
Down Days, 21, 31, 44, 62, 110
Dream Catcher Heliskiing, 57
Durango, 117

E

Eagle Pass Heli Skiing, 58
Easel and Ice, 30
Eastern Europe, vii, 82, 83
Eden, 122, 123
Egans, 33
El Diablo Snowcat Skiing, 116
Elbruz, 89
Elemental Adventure, 18
Equipment, 2, 4, 5
Europe, vii, 21, 82, 83, 96
Everest, 95, 97, 98
Extra vertical, 4

F

Fernie Wilderness Adventures, 58
Film crews, 20, 24, 33, 43
Fisher, Wendy, 33
Fishing, 31, 32, 34, 42, 54
Fog, 23
France, 83, 85, 87, 89, 90, 91, 97
Freeskier Magazine, 24, 27
Freshies, 4, 31

G

Gear, 5, 116
Geneve, 98
Georgia, 84
Girdwood, 2, 31, 32, 38, 42

INDEX

Glacier, 29, 30, 53, 65, 87, 93, 108
Glenorchy, 6
Gloves, 5
Gmoser, Hans, 20
Goggles, 5, 55, 121
Golden, 56, 59, 70
Grand Targhee Resort, 125
Great Northern Snowcat Skiing, 59, 60
Greenland, vii, 92, 93
Greenland Heliskiing, 93
Grizzly Lake Cat Skiing, 60
Guides, 5, 8, 24, 29, 30, 31, 33, 35, 38, 49, 50, 55, 64, 69, 72, 74, 83, 85, 91, 97, 99, 103, 104, 109, 112, 119, 123, 126
Guiding, 8, 33, 38, 83, 85, 91, 99, 104, 123
Gulmarg, 99

H

H2O Heli Guides, 39
Haines, 2, 36, 37, 79
Haines Junction, 79
Hamre, Dave, 2, 31
Harris Mountains Heli-Ski, 106
Heli pad, 6, 7, 49
Heli Ski Queenstown, 106
Helicopter, 2, 7, 8, 21, 28, 30, 33, 37, 38, 44, 62, 67, 72, 84, 86, 87, 90, 104, 123
Helicopter skiing, 2, 33, 72
Heliski Cervinia, 85
Heliski Greenland, 93
Heliski Valgrisenche, 87
Heliskiing, 3, 5, 20, 22, 24, 40, 42, 54, 58, 67, 70, 75, 77, 79, 80, 86, 94, 95, 100, 105, 106, 107, 109, 113, 118, 120
High Mountain Heli-Skiing, 126
Highland Powder Skiing, 60
HighSky Adventures, 60
Himalaya, 96, 97, 98
Himalaya Heliski Kashmir, 98
Himalayan Heliski Guides, 97
Himalayas, vii, 95, 98
Himichal Helicopter Skiing, 96
Huck, 21
Hugo Harrison, 21

I

Idaho, 118, 119, 120

India, 99
Invermere, 73
Island Lake Lodge Catskiing, 61
Italy, 82, 83, 85, 87, 88, 91

J

Jackson Air Force, 33
Jeltema, Jeff, 43, 48
Jensen, Kirk, 2, 33
Juneau, 29, 79

K

Kamchatka, vii, 16, 17
Kashmir, 98, 99
Kashmir Powdercats, 99
Kelly, Craig, 2
Klondike Heliskiing, 61
Kramer, Kirsten, 33
Kreitler, Kent, 33

L

La Thuile, 87, 88
Lamoille, 121
Last Frontier Heliskiing, 61
Leadville, 115
Lighting Ridge Snowcat Skiing, 123
Lodge, 5, 20, 21, 22, 23, 25, 26, 29, 30, 31, 32, 34, 43, 44, 54, 59, 62, 64, 65, 67, 71, 74, 78, 116
Loveland, Shannon, 33
Lyons, Noel, 33

M

Manali, 96
Matchstick Productions, 43
McCall, 118
McClune, 33
McConkey, Shane, 33
Meadow Creek, 60, 76, 81
Methven Heliskiing, 107
Mica Creek, 20
Mica Heli Guides, 20, 43, 44, 45, 46, 47, 48, 62
Michelfelder, Jay, 21
Mike Wiegele Helicopter Skiing, 63

Miller, Warren, 2, 3, 30, 32, 35, 40, 49, 50, 66, 72
Mirkwood, 26
Moe, Tommy, 31, 32
Molas Pass, 116
Monarch, vii, 25, 26, 27, 116
Monarch Mountain, 116
Monarch Pass, 25
Monarch Ski Area, 25
Monarch Snowcat Tours, 25, 116
Monashee, 20, 49, 63, 64, 65, 70
Monashee Powder Adventures, 64
Monashee Powder Snowcats, 63, 64
Montana, 120, 121
Montana Backcountry Adventures, 121
Monterosa Express, 88
Morrison, Seth, 33
Mount Cook, 108, 109
Mountain Terrain, 20, 74
Mountaineer, 86
Mountains, 17, 20, 21, 29, 30, 33, 42, 68, 72, 76, 78, 86, 98, 109, 116, 120
Mt. Larkins, 7
Mt. Potts Backcountry, 107
Mustang Powder Lodge, 64

N

Nelson, 53, 78, 79, 81
Nepal, 97
Nevada, 121
New Delhi, 96
New Denver, 71
New Zealand, vii, 6, 9, 10, 11, 12, 13, 14, 15, 100, 103, 104, 105, 106, 107, 108, 109
Nobis, Jeremy, 32
North America, 38, 69, 123, 126
North Cascade Heli-Skiing, 125
North Elysian, 26
North Powder, 122
Northern Escape Heli-Skiing, 65
Northern Lights, 29
Norwegians, 22

O

Olympics, 22
Operators, 3, v, 5, 7, 43, 44, 58, 82, 113
Orca Lodge, 30
Orca River, 29

Oregon, 122
Overcast, Mike, 2, 31, 32

P

Pacific Crest Snowcats, 115
Pacific Ocean, 16, 17
Pantheon Helisports, 66, 67
Park City, 123
Park City Powder Cats & Heli-Ski, 123
Peace Reach Heli Ski, 67, 68
Peak Adventures Snowcat Skiing, 119
Pehota, Eric, 2, 33
Pemberton, 57
Petersen, Trevor, 33
Petropavlovsk, 17
Petterson, Trevor, 2
Pillow-lines, 23
Pilots, 21, 30, 86, 109
Pitch, 22, 23, 26
Points North, 29, 30, 39, 40
Points North Heli-Adventures, 39
Poliana, Krasnaya, 89
Powder, 5, 7, 8, 17, 22, 23, 29, 41, 42, 44, 55, 62, 63, 64, 67, 68, 69, 71, 72, 73, 75, 76, 77, 89, 90, 93, 96, 100, 105, 108, 110, 112, 115, 116, 117, 118, 120, 121, 123, 124, 126
Powder Cowboy Catskiing, 69
Powder Mountain Winter Resort, 123
Powder Outfitters, 69
Powder South Heliski Guides, 112
Prince William Sound, 29, 34
Private charter, 103, 104, 106
Purcell Helicopter Skiing, 70

Q

Queenstown, 6, 7, 100, 103, 104, 106, 108, 109
Quinn, Kevin, 2, 29

R

Rain forest, 29, 62
Raynor, Scott, 33, 34
Retallack Alpine Adventures, 71
Revelstoke, 20, 56, 58, 59, 62, 65, 75
Ridge, 7, 22, 23, 72, 97
RK Heliski, 73
Robson HeliMagic, 75

INDEX

Rossland, 54, 78
Ruby Mountain Helicopterskiing, 121
Russia, vii, 16, 89
Rutor Glacier, 87

S

Salida, 26, 27
San Juan Ski Company, 117
Sandpoint, 119
Santiago, 111
Schmidt, Scot, 2, 25, 33
Seattle, 29, 79, 124
Selkirk, 20, 59, 71, 73, 75, 76, 119
Selkirk Mountains, 59, 71
Selkirk Powder Company, 119
Selkirk Tangiers Heli Skiing, 75
Selkirk Wilderness Skiing, 76
Skeena Heliskiing, 77
Ski Anthony Lakes, 122
Ski movies, 26, 121
Ski The Tasman, 108
Smithers, 77
Snow, 6, 7, 17, 21, 22, 23, 25, 26, 27, 30, 31, 32, 41, 42, 44, 49, 54, 55, 58, 62, 63, 67, 70, 71, 72, 73, 75, 76, 83, 85, 86, 87, 88, 90, 91, 93, 96, 98, 99, 103, 104, 105, 107, 108, 110, 111, 116, 118, 121, 123, 124, 125
Snowbird, 124
Snowcat, v, 25, 27, 31, 39, 55, 56, 60, 63, 64, 65, 69, 72, 77, 78, 81, 99, 108, 116, 121, 123
SnowCat Adventures, 125
Snowcat Skiing, 60, 117
Snowwater Heli Skiing, 78
South America, vii, 110, 111
South Island, 100, 107, 108, 109
Southern Alps, 6, 98, 104, 106, 108
Southern Lakes Heliski, 108, 109
Squamish, 66
Steamboat Powdercats, 117
Steamboat Springs, 117
Sun Peaks, 60
Sun Valley, 120
Sun Valley Heli Ski Guides, 120
Swanwick, David, 33
Sweden, 89, 90
Switzerland, 83, 84, 85, 90, 91

T

Tahoe, 36, 115
Tahoe City, 36, 115
Tasman Glacier, 105, 108
Telluride, 117
Telluride Helitrax, 117
Terrace, 65
Terrain, 1, 5, 6, 7, 21, 22, 23, 24, 25, 26, 27, 29, 32, 36, 37, 38, 40, 42, 43, 53, 54, 55, 59, 62, 63, 65, 66, 67, 69, 70, 71, 72, 74, 75, 76, 78, 80, 89, 93, 97, 103, 104, 105, 106, 107, 109, 110, 112, 113, 115, 116, 120, 123
Teton Gravity Research, 43
Teton Village, 126
TGR, 33
The Zells, 33
Thompson Pass, 1, 33, 37, 38, 42
Tipping, 4
TLH Heliskiing, 78
Totalskidskolan, 89
Treadway, Dan, 21
Treeline, 21, 22, 23, 25
Tree-skiing, 23
Tsania, 1, 33
Tulsequah Heliskiing, 79
Turkey, 91
Turkey Heliski, 91

U

Ulmer, Kristen, 33
United States, 2, vii, 113, 115, 120
Utah, 122

V

Vacation, 5, 68, 113, 119
Vail, 118
Vail Snowcat Skiing, 118
Valdez, 1, 2, 29, 31, 32, 33, 34, 35, 37, 38, 39, 41, 42
Valdez Heli Camps, 41
Valdez Heli Ski Guides, 2, 34, 42
Valemount, 75
Valhalla Powdercats, 79
Vancouver, 24
Vanderhoof, 57
Verbier, 91
Vernon, 60, 61, 64, 78

Vertical quota, 4
Viaggi, Lyskamm, 88
Vienna, 22

W

Wanaka, 6, 103, 104, 105, 109
Wanrooy, Bill, 1, 3, 8, 44, 47, 48
Wasatch Powderbird Guides, 124
Washington, 119, 124, 125
Wax, Lisa, 33
Weather, 4, 6, 7, 17, 21, 24, 25, 28, 31, 32, 36, 49, 54, 62, 74, 76, 80, 96, 107, 116, 126
Westbridge, 69
Wheately, Spencer, 35
Whiskey, 6, 22
Whistler, 23, 53, 54, 66, 80
Whistler Heli-Skiing, 80

White Grizzly Cat Skiing, 81
Whitefish, 120
Wilderness Heliskiing, 109
Wildhorse Snowcat Skiing, 81
Winthrop, 125
Woodinville, 124
World Extreme Skiing Championships, 31, 33, 38
Wyoming, 125

Y

Yak & Yeti Services, 89

Z

Zermatt, 90

Printed in the United States
60177LVS00007B/82